T0317727

John Fuller

& the Sycamore Press

John Fuller
& the Sycamore Press

A bibliographic history

COMPILED AND EDITED BY
RYAN ROBERTS

Bodleian Library
UNIVERSITY OF OXFORD

First published in 2010 by

The Bodleian Library
Broad Street, Oxford OX1 3BG
www.bodleianbookshop.co.uk

and

Oak Knoll Press
310 Delaware Street,
New Castle, DE 19720, USA
www.oakknoll.com

ISBN   978 1 85124 323 5 (UK)
ISBN   978 1 58456 281 8 (USA)

Cover design by Dot Little
Text designed and typeset in Monotype Bulmer by illuminati, Grosmont
Printed in Great Britain by the MPG Books Group, Bodmin and King's Lynn
on 80 gsm Vancouver Cream Bookwove Vol. 18

Mixed Sources
Product group from well-managed
forests, controlled sources and
recycled wood or fiber
www.fsc.org Cert no. TT-COC-002303
© 1996 Forest Stewardship Council
FSC

The FSC logo identifies products that contain wood
from well-managed forests, certified in accordance
with the strict environmental, social and economic
standards of the Forest Stewardship Council

Cataloguing in Publication Data
A CIP record of this publication is available from
the British Library and the Library of Congress

Contents

Our Western Furniture.   James Fent[on]

1968		
9 August	60	Cartridge paper for bound copies
		amount ordered is for total lot = circa 110
"	900+	Blenheim wove 40 lb crown fol[io]
11 Oct	100	Postcards for publicity
30 Oct		Type and art rule for cover
7 Nov		Cover paper
15 Nov		Cartridge paper for endpapers
16 Nov		Postage (9 @ 4$\frac{d}{}$ + 1^d for enve[lope]
29 Nov		Postage for publicity 20 & 4[0]
16 Dec		Postage
"		Postage
15 Feb		Postage
24 April		Postage (to date)
2 July		Charge for binding materials at th[e]
		Ink
2 Jan 70		Postage
6 Jan 70		Postage

Foreword

John Fuller

Now that the Sycamore Press has its own bibliography, and its archives have been acquired by the Bodleian Library of the University of Oxford, it is hard not to think of it as a somehow fully envisaged and decisively executed enterprise. A quarter of a century of literary printing by hand! The notion has a ring of deliberation and conviction. And yet at the time my wife Prue and I launched into the thing pretty much on a whim.

After the birth of our third daughter, Prue was given by an imaginative friend not a bowl of grapes but a book of type. Fired by an old editorializing urge never properly satisfied, and with happy memories of the inky parts of the English Faculty's graduate bibliography course, I rushed out and bought an old Arab clamshell press for £20. It cost rather more to have the broken treadle welded and the whole thing shipped to our garage. Even more to set ourselves up with new Stephenson Blake type and cases, re-cover the rollers, and so on, but we were soon printing. The Arab had formerly produced cricket scores for distribution in the University Parks, and was never meant for more than cards or posters. Nonetheless we cheerfully set about publishing a 36-page booklet imposed in quarto and sewn by hand into a two-colour cover. The typography, the inking and impression, the sewing, the distribution and the discovered errors all became the occasion for obsession or alarm. No worries about the contents, of course, whose composition I had encouraged and felt deserved immediate circulation: it was the Newdigate Prize poem for 1968 on the set subject of the opening of Japan in the 1850s. It was called *Our Western Furniture*, and was James Fenton's first publication.

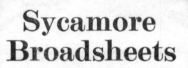

Simultaneously with the Fenton we started a series of broadsheets (actually sheets of foolscap quarto folded to a triptych), each of which would contain a clutch of new poems and sell for 6d (2½p). The idea was to promote the work of unknown poets by bribing subscribers with offerings from quite famous ones. You paid up, and were sent not only Thom Gunn but Glyn Hughes, not only Philip Larkin but Peter Scupham, not only Peter Porter but David Lehman.

The idea still seems to me a good one, but I am forced at this point to confront the perennial dashed hopes of small presses. In general, during the lifetime of a press nobody really wants to buy its titles. No one has heard of its authors except the authors' friends. And if you publish a famous name, then no one quite believes you or loses your address even if they get to hear of you in the first place. For example, there wasn't exactly a rush to buy copies of W.H. Auden's 1937 ballad

Sue, at that time nowhere in print or even in existence other than as Sycamore Broadsheet 23. And who wanted the poems of Alan Hollinghurst when I first published them? I do get orders now that he's famous, but they're probably all from investing bibliophiles (and almost certainly they believe *Confidential Chats with Boys* is as racy as *The Swimming Pool Library* or *The Line of Beauty*). We published 200 copies of *Our Western Furniture* at 5 shillings (25p) a copy, and perhaps thanks to a dramatized reading on the Third Programme (itself a result of my sending producer George MacBeth a copy that proved to be miscollated and therefore that amusing thing, an instant rarity) we did sell out after two years. Now a copy of *Our Western Furniture* has been spotted in a bookseller's catalogue at £300, and the Hollinghurst at $1,300. However, an edition the following year of 400 copies of Norman Bryson's *The Swimmer and Other Poems* has never sold out (I have plenty of copies a quarter of a century later), probably because its student author became a distinguished art historian and not a distinguished poet. My single important piece of advice to would-be small publishers therefore is: whatever you want to print, and whatever your technology, do make sure that you are ready to give a lot of time to publicity and distribution. I never was, and it was a mistake. Once the finished booklet was in my hands (and the poet's twenty-five complimentaries in his or hers) I was happy. Oh yes, I would drive to London and haunt the bookshops, placing half a dozen copies here and there on a sale-or-return basis, but often forgot to return and see what had happened. Fatal.

In my rash technical enthusiasm I found ways to print music, using musical symbols that you rubbed off from sheets of transfer paper (it was called Letraset) and then having zinc line-blocks made. I tried to print linocuts (it was impossible to get a satisfactory impression). Prue learned some bookbinding, and produced a small number of bound copies of *Our Western Furniture* printed on thicker paper. I even made my own paper and printed on it, despite its being unsized, of varying thickness and generally as rough in texture as egg cartons. But the main point of what we were doing was, of course, to publish new poetry.

I suppose my immediate role model was Oscar Mellor's Fantasy Press, one of the very last publications of which, *Oxford Poetry* (1960), I had edited. Oscar had the distinction of having published Gunn, Amis, Larkin, Jennings and others in the 1950s; I admired both his taste and his chaste typography. If I had had the time and energy I would have tried to publish more of the new poets of the 1970s and 1980s. As it is, I am proud to have acted as booklet-midwife to the emerging James Fenton, Mick Imlah, Bernard O'Donoghue, Alan Hollinghurst, Mark Wormald, Gerard Woodward and others (including members of the John Florio Society of Magdalen, who helped with the production of three collections of their work during the 1980s). Setting type by hand is laborious, and it was never more than a weekend activity, a booklet taking almost a year to produce. Typesetting sometimes seemed to be little more than an excuse for gossipy lunches; getting an edition sewn and guillotined often needed the bribery of stiff vodkatinis. And having sometimes to machine on into the dusk by lamplight seemed a romantic thing to be doing.

My haphazard technical skills must have irritated my poets. No proofs, of course, since once I was inked up I couldn't bear to stop. If the author could be around to correct the text during machining, so much the better: stiffer vodkatinis were in order. (I never had a good enough bribe for the dismal process of distributing type.) Sometimes terrible things happened, as on the occasion when I ran out of the letter *f* while setting a particularly clotted double-spread of Mick Imlah's poem about Quasimodo (a loquacious dramatic monologue: the completed forme seemed to weigh about as much as a small car). My simple solution (at least, it seemed simple to me) was to ask him to rewrite the poem here and there, losing two or three *f*s. I now marvel that he was willing to do so, turning 'foul as water' to 'pale as water' and so on. On the other hand, I can't imagine what the alternative would have been. We couldn't wait for weeks while I ordered more type. Nor could I be bothered to reprint a whole impression of a Fenton broadsheet when I got the title wrong (the actual *title*!).

MICK IMLAH

The Zoologist's Bath and other adventures

Sycamore Press

The letterpress printer with dirty fingers scouring his empty *f* box, getting a locked knee from treadling and callouses from sewing, is closely and wonderfully in touch with his craft, even if he is as lazy as I was. The same goes for the hypnosis of composing: you remember the line as you set it, you remember it back-to-front and upside-down, you jolly well curse it when you find you haven't minded your *p*s and *q*s (though with me it always seemed to be *n*s and *h*s) and you find you remember it as you distribute it. You do rather have to like a poem to do all that. I loved them all, and am still haunted by them in ways that I am never haunted by poems I have simply *read*.

Introduction

Ryan Roberts

The Sycamore Press began in 1968, when John Fuller purchased an Arab platen press for £20. While the press eventually published some of the most respected poets of its time, including Philip Larkin, W.H. Auden, Thom Gunn and Peter Porter (to name a few), the first item Fuller printed was an eight-line verse titled 'Robbers', written by his young daughter. While not itemized as an 'official' publication of the press, the poem represents the underlying philosophy of the Sycamore Press — to cultivate the talents of young poets.

In order to promote new or less-known poets, Fuller created the Sycamore Press's Broadsheet series. As he claims in his foreword to this volume, 'The idea was to promote the work of unknown poets by bribing subscribers with offerings from quite famous ones.' By mentoring and encouraging poetic exploration by numerous poets, many of them previously untested, Fuller helped shape the literary scene for years to come. James Fenton, Alan Hollinghurst, David Lehman, Elise Paschen, Mark Wormald, Mick Imlah, David Harsent and many others found their way to Fuller's press, and all would, in one form or another, make their own mark on the literary world.

As the author contributions included in this volume reveal, Fuller was a trusted critic of poetry drafts. Both new and established poets deferred to his judgement on matters of editing and re-crafting poems. Bernard O'Donoghue, who published *Razorblades and Pencils* with the Sycamore Press and was a regular contributor to the John Florio Society pamphlets the press produced, says, 'John has extraordinary editorial gifts, evident at Florio meetings as well as in the printing process.' Glyn Hughes acknowledges that Fuller helped him 'a good deal with the poems that eventually became my first book with a major house'. In a letter accompanying three potential Sycamore poems, Peter Porter writes, 'I know you won't hesitate to tell me if you think it's too poor to use.' But perhaps Elise Paschen states it best in her contribution:

> John was an incredible mentor and editor. He championed and supported our poetry — from encouraging us to write new poems for the Florio Society to editing and publishing our work. He was brilliant and funny, generous and kind. I was honored to be counted among the poets John selected and privileged to be included in his company.

Booker Prize-winner Alan Hollinghurst echoes Paschen's praise and admiration when he writes, 'John's encouragement was essential to the years in which I was trying to be a poet: he read and commented on almost everything I wrote and by publishing some of it made my name known to a few interested readers, while opening up in me a sense of the possibility of becoming a writer.'

In addition to thirty items in the Sycamore Press's Broadsheet series, Fuller published a significant number of poetry pamphlets. The Press's first pamphlet publication was also the author's first — James Fenton's *Our Western Furniture*. A complicated production set in quarto, the book was one of several attempts to stretch the capabilities of Fuller's Arab press. When Anthony Furnivall set a Mallarmé poem to music, Fuller was 'intrigued' by the 'interesting technical challenge' of publishing music on such a small press: 'normally music is quite big — you prop it up on the piano and look at it from a distance. That was the largest size I could do getting those blocks into my forme, which is quite small.'

Similar experiments were attempted in some of the Sycamore Cards Fuller published in the 1970s. In one instance, Fuller printed circular staves of music, while for another card he used moveable chess type to reconstruct a game played between Morphy and the Duke of Brunswick. Fuller included original illustrations in a number of these cards, including an excellent drawing by Julian Bell for Card No. 1, *Corncrake*, and he produced a series of cards featuring linocuts by Brigette Hanf for a more formal publication of a Bestiary, with short verses written by Fuller for each card.

As with all writers and poets, John Fuller's reputation rests with the quality of his published works, and in this regard he is highly respected as a poet, novelist and scholar. But his writings are not the only measure of Fuller's impact on the literary world. As this bibliographical history confirms, Fuller's years of devotion to the Sycamore Press reveal a new aspect of his importance as a mentor and editor of some of the finest poets and writers of the mid- to late twentieth century.

When I first contacted John Fuller about compiling a biblio-graphical history of the Sycamore Press, he was immediately open to the idea. I visited his home in May 2006, and he graciously allowed me to borrow the ledger book he used to keep track of

Sycamore Press publications, press expenditures and sales. He also provided a large number of specimen copies, both broadsheets and pamphlets, which, added to numerous items provided by Julian Barnes, served as the primary examination copies for the bibliography. In March 2007 I returned to Oxford for a week's research in Fuller's Sycamore Press archive. I met with John at his home in Oxford to discuss the Sycamore Press, and an edited transcript of our conversation is included at the end of this volume.

In February 2007 I sent letters to twenty-eight authors published by Sycamore Press requesting contributions of their remembrances and reflections on John Fuller and their experiences with the Press. It is a testament to John's importance to British poetry and to his generous personality that so many Sycamore authors replied with such enthusiasm.

The core of this book rests with the Sycamore Press's output, with the poems that John Fuller laboured to publish on his Arab press. The bibliography provides full bibliographical descriptions of all known Sycamore Press booklets, broadsheets, cards, promotional items and ephemera.

Several notes between John and Prue Fuller survive in the Sycamore Press archive. These exchanges serve as examples of the couple's collaboration on the press, especially in decisions regarding the selection of texts to publish. John is quick to give Prue her proper credit, and the archive supports his depiction of her keen editorial eye. The Sycamore Press ledger book provides a tremendous amount of detailed information regarding print runs, paper types and publication dates. Such information is included in the bibliography whenever possible.

✳

Special thanks are due to John and Prue Fuller for all their assistance and helpfulness during the compilation of this bibliography. Without their kind offer of time, memories, and countless specimens from the Sycamore Press archive, this project would never have been completed.

I am forever indebted to James Fenton for his generosity and friendship throughout this project, for introducing me to the Fullers, and for hosting my two research trips to Oxford. I greatly cherish his care and support from beginning to end. Thanks also to Darryl Pinckney for his kindness during various stages of this bibliography. My great appreciation is also extended to Julian Barnes for his friendship, encouragement, and for providing me with numerous Sycamore Press specimens from his personal collection.

Thanks to Lincoln Land Community College for granting me a semester sabbatical to compile the bibliography, to Eileen Tepatti for her unswerving support, and to the Faculty Development & Recognition Committee for funding that supported my travel to Oxford. Of the several booksellers I contacted in search of Sycamore Press items, two were of particular help: Joe McCann of Maggs Bros, London; and Seamus Cooney of Celery City Books, Michigan.

I am grateful for the opportunity to work with Lucy Morton of illuminati books and the tremendously helpful Samuel Fanous, Deborah Susman and Chris Fletcher at the Bodleian Library. It has been a privilege to work with them and reassuring to know they were shepherding this text to publication.

This bibliography is dedicated to my loving wife Tricia, without whom this and numerous other projects would never have seen the light of day.

Authors' contributions

Julian Bell

Illustrator, *Corncrake* (1973), with Andrew McNeillie

In 1973 I was a twenty-year-old Eng Lit undergraduate who probably should have been at art school rather than at Magdalen, and Andrew the immensely senior twenty-four(?)-year-old colleague with a passion to introduce interesting poetry to his friends — above all that of Geoffrey Hill. *Corncrake* was one among many vivid and wiry poems he showed me at the time, most still unpublished. When Andrew passed on John Fuller's Sycamore Press idea for poem-cards, I walked up to the Pitt Rivers (with Andrew? I don't remember) and asked if they'd got a specimen of such a legendary beast. I waited about among the saurians and gothickry and in due course someone came up from the vaults, handing me a smallish dun weightless object, soft to the touch but very dead, which he assured me was a bona fide ex-*Crex crex*. I propped it on some volumes of Milton or something and drew, trying to reanimate it. I bunged in a suggestion of stone walls, taken from the Cotswold stone walls you have about Oxford, behind it.

John was my tutor for some of the time and above all I remember the sensation of the great armchair in his rooms in New Buildings. To sit in it was rather like collapsing arse-first into an enormous bucket, for it had no springs and one felt, as one's limbs poked and thrashed upwards, that its seat must have fallen some way below floor-level. I had belted down the stairs of the New Buildings frantically as Magdalen Tower struck ten, it was Tuesday morning and the weekly essay was due. Having invited me to sink into this prone position, John would habitually present me with a glass of Bulmer's No. 7, before bearing with my reading of my verbiage. This is to say that the whole experience was radically giddy, and rather delightful; and whatever it was John had to say contributed to the sensation of benign delirium.

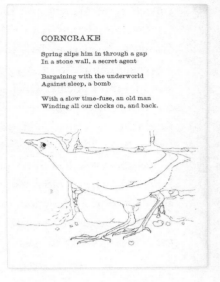

CORNCRAKE

Spring slips him in through a gap
In a stone wall, a secret agent

Bargaining with the underworld
Against sleep, a bomb

With a slow time-fuse, an old man
Winding all our clocks on, and back.

Bernard Bergonzi

Memorials (1970)

In 1955 I entered Wadham College, Oxford, as a youngish mature student of twenty-six, to read English. I wrote poetry myself and made contact with other Oxford poets, among them John Fuller, then an undergraduate at New College.

We became good friends and both entered academic life after graduating. For a short time we were both teaching at the

University of Manchester; then in 1966 John left to return to Oxford, and I moved to the newly established University of Warwick. A few years later John asked me if I had any poems for a Sycamore broadsheet. My output of poetry had declined, but I sent him three poems, which appeared as *Memorials*, Broadsheet no. 11, in 1970. I can't remember anything about the process of production except that it went smoothly. In 1979 I reprinted two of them, 'East, West' and '21st July 1969', in a collection of sixteen poems called *Years* published by the Mandeville Press. John and I do not often meet these days, but we keep in touch and in 2002 he gave me some valuable information for a biography I was writing, *A Victorian Wanderer: The Life of Thomas Arnold the Younger* (OUP, 2003).

Alan Brownjohn

Woman Reading Aloud (1969)

The Sycamore Press followed in the post-war tradition established by Oscar Mellor and his Fantasy Press of printing and publishing poems in small editions, finely printed in a way that delighted both poets and readers. The poets felt pleased to be asked and knew that the production would be handsomely unfussy.

Somewhere or other in a cluttered flat I have a small suitcase of small-press publications and among them, unsorted, are numerous examples of John's labours. I suppose my contribution must have been one of the earliest. It was a poem called 'Woman Reading Aloud' and it consisted of 100 short lines done somewhat in the style of the Black Mountain poets. That influenced me at the time to the extent of having three poems of that length in the book I published in 1972 called *Warrior's Career*. But later

I took against 'Woman Reading Aloud' and did not include it in my editions of *Collected Poems*; so it could only be tracked down now in the Sycamore version or in *Warrior's Career*, itself a rare book because one printing of it had to be redone for fear of a libel action and subsequently many copies were lost in a warehouse fire.

I went on collecting Sycamore Press publications, which seemed to arrive regularly through the 1970s, and the last one I have to hand is *Iron Aspidistra*, by Mark Members, in 1985. I was then, and still am, a huge fan of the novels of Anthony Powell and was delighted to make acquaintance with this famous poem in Powell's *A Question of Upbringing*. Producing this (fictitious) poem for Sycamore was, of course, the work of John's father, Roy Fuller — the poem did not previously exist until Sycamore published it for Anthony Powell's eightieth birthday.

I never actually saw the press itself, but I have believed for years that it was, like the Fantasy Press and the Mandeville Press, in the equivalent of the editor's garage. Or perhaps his actual garage? Garage poetry seems to me a very honourable genre, and hardly ever a junk project, as in the case of the music to which the same adjective is attached.

Ian Caws

Cathy's Clutter (1978)

In the 1960s and '70s, I was very interested in the private press movement (I attended Loughborough School of Librarianship for a year in the mid-1960s and had my enthusiasm kindled by Roderick Cave, an influential figure in the private press world and then a lecturer at Loughborough).

Three factors may have led me to approach the Sycamore Press — John Fuller was (and is) a poet I much admire, I read somewhere that the Sycamore Press was run from his garage (which appealed), and poets like James Fenton and Andrew Motion were publishing there.

In 1978, I was moving towards my first full-length collection, *Boy with a Kite* (Sidgwick & Jackson, 1981), which John Fuller was kind enough to review in the *Observer* and which included 'Cathy's Clutter'.

Douglas Dunn

Corporal Punishment (1975)

As well as contributing a poem (which I seem to have lost, or else it's buried in my archives) I subscribed to the series. It was always a pleasure to receive these pamphlets. I could tell from John's handwriting what was in the envelope. One I especially remember was Larkin's Baudelairean *Femmes Damnées*.

Pamphlet and chapbook publishing seems to be undergoing something of a revival. There's a fine series edited by a friend of mine in this part of Scotland, Helena Nelson, called Happenstance.

I'm afraid I can remember little or next to nothing of writing *Corporal Punishment*. It's likely to have been a poem of appropriate length which I happened to have available.

James Fenton

Our Western Furniture (1968)
Put Thou Thy Tears into My Bottle (1969)
The Sycamore Miscellany (1977)
Dead Soldiers (1981)

Some twenty years after the Sycamore Press was founded, I was living in a country where, if you wanted art of any kind, you had to shift for yourself. If you wanted a good book, you had to get on a plane to Hong Kong or Seoul. Likewise if you wanted to hear classical music. Or see something other than the local brand of cheap and cheerful film.

Young writers in this place were in the habit of sitting around bemoaning the paucity of literary opportunities. There were few magazines or literary publishers, and you had to be one of a tiny elite to see your work in print. I used to say to some would-be poets I knew that, if they wanted to have their work published, the best thing would be to publish it themselves. The best way to get into print would be to print their own poems.

These would-be poets reacted with some fastidious distrust. Surely, they thought, if you printed things yourself, that wouldn't count as genuine publishing. Surely only a professional publisher would do for the writing career they had in mind — a career that would stretch from Quezon City to the Iowa Writers' Workshops and beyond, to Manhattan fame.

Throughout such desolate conversations, I became aware that this notorious paucity of Filipino publishing houses and magazines had become a very good excuse for not writing anything at all. And so I set to work to explain that, where I came from, no stigma at all attached itself to self-publishing and the small presses. On the contrary. A great small press was a much-loved thing. It had been part of my luck as a writer to be published by two such outfits, one of them (the Sycamore Press) run by my university tutor, the other (the Salamander Press) by my brother.

But this information only fed the incredulity of my listeners. It appeared impossible to convey anything of the romance of the small press, the daydream quality, the vision of craft and self-sufficiency. When English poets think of a great small-press book, what comes to mind is Auden's first collection of poems, created by Stephen Spender with equipment designed for printing labels, and in an edition fantastically small. There is for us a profound sense of honour involved in such enterprises. Nothing in mass market production can come close to it.

Both the Sycamore and the Salamander Press began life in garages. John Fuller and his wife Prue had bought a new house in Oxford near Lady Margaret Hall, in a handsome modernist development where each home had two lock-up spaces. The possession of an extra garage, surplus to requirements, had set them thinking. The space was enough for a press and its accoutrements — the rollers, the trays of type, the ink, and so forth. Really it served its purpose extraordinarily well, although the garage door had to be kept open when work was in progress.

In the first instance, John's ambition reached only so far as a series of poetry broadsheets. In this series, student work appeared in the same list as that of established writers, just as in John and Prue's parties we (the students) were able to rub shoulders with well-known names.

The publication of poetry suits the amateur printer very well. Most poems consist of rather few words, and the lines are usually only justified to the left, not to left and right. One is spared a part of that minuscule labour of filling out the line so that the words appear evenly spaced. But no traditional printer is spared the tedious business of redistributing the type — putting the letters back in their proper compartments in the tray.

The trays themselves, and the old printers' blocks, began appearing, during these years, in certain kinds of antique shop or junk stall, as more and more of the old printing houses closed down. They became functionless curiosities. This phase was followed by a fashion for imitation trays — the antique market must have exhausted the supply of the real thing. But at the time that the Sycamore Press was first operating it was still possible to find letterpress print-shops in small towns, serving a need not for books but for small-scale items such as church service sheets.

From letterpress to Linotype and on — in a short period I must have learned and been obliged to work with every progressive stage of printing technology until, around the time of my conversations with the would-be poets in the Philippines, we all graduated to the computer. And I often think, when my eye wanders to the top of my computer screen, of the extraordinary facility represented by those four adjacent squares which allow you to decide, at a mere touch, whether to justify to left, to centre, to right or to left and right. And I think of all those little slivers of lead.

For the Newdigate Prize in 1968, I wrote a poem in which I was determined to use all the 300 maximum lines that the judges allowed. I made a plan to write 21 sonnets which would be divided into three sets of seven. The six lines left over could be two haiku. So the poem went seven sonnets — haiku — seven sonnets — haiku — seven sonnets. The middle sonnet of the middle section, the central sonnet of the poem, had a rhyme scheme which went A B C D E F G –G F E D C B A: a chiasmus.

John decided to go through all the labour of printing it, and Prue, who had just taken classes in bookbinding, undertook to bind a small hardback version. My prize poem was published, and, on the back of the publication, was broadcast on the Third Programme, and the actor who had played the Sheriff of

Nottingham in the children's television series of *Robin Hood* took one of the voices.

What a launch in life! What luck! And what a setting forth! And what a strangely constructed vehicle it was that drove out of John's garage that day.

Alastair Fowler

Seventeen (1971)
Helen's Topless Towers (1975)

Seventeen is among my earliest published verse. I remember John being very generous with his time, for example in showing me how to revise verse for publication. Twelve of the poems

in *Seventeen* were reprinted in *Catacomb Suburb* (Edinburgh University Press, 1976) as part of a section called 'Bits'. Nine new poems were added, making twenty-one in all.

'Helen's Topless Towers' also appeared in *Catacomb Suburb*, as no. 3 of a section of eight poems titled 'Towers', all but one of them shape or concrete poems.

Richard Gordon-Freeman

Swimming 1949 (1980)

In April 1975 John Fuller saw a batch of my poems and wrote, 'I much approve the humour and observation of these poems, and the rhythm and tone.' He continued, 'We both have a thing about surfaces of water but you've got it properly into your poems. It's still only in my nightmares.' Then came an invitation, 'Perhaps you have some new poems? I have a little printing press...'

I am a slow poet, in every sense, and we now shuffle forwards to 1978 when Anthony Whittome, an editor at Hutchinson, and a friend, offered this comment when rejecting a collection of mine, 'The best of the serious poems is, I think, *Swimming 1949*, and I hope you will write more in this vein.' By March 1980, five years after our first contact, the poem *Swimming 1949* had reached John Fuller and to my great surprise he remembered who I was. He replied, 'The poem is beautifully paced and recounted, with excellent detail.' He considered it would suit the broadsheet format well.

In those days, John sent contributors forty or so poems to sell, while he recouped some of his costs by selling copies on subscription, and eventually, in October 1980, my copies arrived, with a note from John explaining that there had been some delay because the press had broken down. Naturally I was pleased to see my poem in print, and as John had predicted, it fitted the space well.

Another note followed unexpectedly soon. Just two weeks later, with an amusing covering note, John sent me a copy of a letter he had received from an irate subscriber. The writer said, 'I regret I shall not be renewing my subscription to Sycamore Press Broadsheets'. He added, 'Instead of churning out yards of this drivel you could do a real service to poetry by starting a revival of satire.' He then refers to a line in my poem, 'Honestly "empty as a slice of bread" — why not "as empty as a Sycamore Broadsheet?"'

Many, one could say most, poets have a thing about water. In his poem 'Annie Upside Down' John wrote about 'the dark pool in the wood where the eels make no noise'. My obsession

Richard Freeman

Swimming 1949

Sycamore Broadsheet 29

began when I nearly drowned at Laleham ferry. I was about five years old, and was fished out by the ferryman, who, thank God, happened to be on the water at the time, and heard my brother's shouts for help. A couple of years later, in 1945, I was taught to swim at the same spot, by a German prisoner of war who was allowed to work in our small garden, in return for cigarettes.

The village youngsters used to swim together a lot, and we had our favourite places. The landing stage I wrote about was one of them. But one day, treading water, I discovered a rotted, pointed wooden stake below the surface. It would have skewered any one of us who had accidentally jumped or dived onto it, and the wound would probably have been horrific, even fatal. This was an unforgettable childhood experience with nightmare qualities; we are on the edge of 'the dark pool in the wood where the eels make no noise'.

Of course, I would not be sharing any of this with you were it not for John Fuller and his 'little printing press'. And where would poetry be without people like John? On the one hand, he is an enormously skilful and intriguing poet to whom poetry clearly means everything, and, on the other hand, he is an enormously skilful and intriguing poet to whom poetry clearly means everything.

I'm writing this in France. Here, to a man like John, you say 'Chapeau'.

Thom Gunn

The Fair in the Woods (1969)

975 Filbert St.,
San Francisco,
Calif 94133
18 April 1969

Dear John,

I received all the copies of the pamphlet the day before yester-
day. Thank you — it looks very nice indeed. I'm most happy to
be in your series.

Interesting what you say about the poem. I hate notes to
poems, but maybe I have withheld more information about the
situation than is fair to the reader. I suppose it's clear enough
that it's about taking an acid trip at some kind of a fair. But the
fair was a rather nice thing that is held in the country every year
and is called the Renaissance Fair. People dress up slightly in
cross garters, makeshift cowls and doublets and things. Mead and
such things are sold. There are jugglers, etc. It may sound rather
repulsively pretentious, but nobody who goes to it ever thinks so
— it is quite relaxed and pleasant. Anyway, all the things in the
poem were actual. The man on the horse, the dancer and the rest
of her group. And people at fairs, pop music festivals, sit ins and
be ins etc., always seem to be getting into trees (see Genet on the
Chicago Conventions).

I suppose I was trying to have it both ways, first for it to work
as fairly literal description for anybody who was with me tripping
at the fair (but description meant to be charged with luminosity,
tho I think that's mixing metaphors a bit), and secondly for it to
work as a kind of vision poem. And I don't know that the reader
needs to know the *source* of a vision for a poem about it to work.

'Kubla Khan' doesn't need Coleridge's note, after all. But of course my poem is not really 'Kubla Khan'!

Anyway, thank you for doing it.

Best,
Thom

David Harsent

Ashridge (1969)
Truce (1973)
Storybook Hero (1992)

I was working in a bookshop in the late 1960s and first became
aware of the Sycamore Press when a little wire carousel was
installed on a counter-top to hold a number of Sycamore broadsheets. It also, at one stage, held copies of the first issue of Ian
Hamilton's *The Review* so, clearly, the bookshop's owner (though
I remember him, unjustly it would seem, as a middlebrow con-
servative) was prepared to take a risk both on poetry and on
garage publishing.

In fact, it was through Ian Hamilton that I first met John; this
was later — around the time of my first book, I would think. I
liked John's work and trusted his judgement (still do, still would)
and it was a privilege to join the Sycamore list. The title poem
of my broadsheet, 'Ashridge', was a lament for a friend whose
death by misadventure I had (in life as well as in art) dramatized
into suicide. When I wrote to James Fenton, from London, for a
copy of his *Manila Envelope* it came to me with an accompanying
letter in which he said, 'I thought you lived in Ashridge.' I didn't,
but I wanted to: not the place itself so much as an Ashridge of
the mind, where colours were muted, the wind sour and things
stood at risk.

My first Sycamore pamphlet, *Truce*, spun a little narrative
off some loaded (for me anyway) images. The poem wasn't personal in the sense of autobiographical, but derived, in part, from
personal issues. Projection has always been part of the game for
me. I've written, often, in sequences, using a lyrical vocabulary
to provide (I hope) intense moments from a part-hidden narrative, and this was an early example. I seem to have been taken

by notions of a sort of home-grown decadence at the time: in relationships, in attitudes, in outward instances such as clothing or deliberately sculpted speech. The poem appeared in a collection called *Dreams of the Dead*, and there's another sequence in that book — 'Moments in the Lifetime of Milady' — that I think of as a sort of companion piece. (I wonder who they were, those women with their silks, their exotica, their past follies, their feverish quotidian, their expectation of loss...)

I'm unforgivably lousy at keeping correspondence — among my losses are letters from Ted Hughes, Philip Larkin, Romola Nijinsky... and John Fuller; but I think I remember getting a letter from John saying how much he liked *Truce* and letting me have details of format, the colour of the cover (mustard yellow), that the title would be in green, and mentioning that the booklet would be bound (that is, sewn) with string hand-dyed green to match the title. That kind of care was always lavished on Sycamore publications.

I've recently discovered (or been reminded) that *Storybook Hero*, a pamphlet, and my third Sycamore title, was the Press's last. It's dated 1992. It is beautifully produced: heavy board cover, string dyed red to match, and luxurious cream-coloured paper. In yet another lost letter (writing this, I realise how stupidly careless I have been and am suddenly stricken by regret) John wrote telling me about the illustration on the front. Lacking the letter that would solve its mystery, all I can say is that it looks like a man, arms raised and about to strike two large drums dependent from a neck-brace. Maybe that's what it is.

The pamphlet is dedicated to Harrison Birtwistle. I wrote the libretto for his opera *Gawain*, which opened at the Royal Opera House in the 1990/91 season, and the poem has about it a flavour of that piece: certainly the notion of hubris earning a harsh reward. At the end of the opera, chivvied by Arthur and others in the court to brag of his adventures, Gawain turns from them and sings, 'I'm not that hero'. Echoes of that bleak, virtuous and (for the Arthurian court) destructive confession are in 'Storybook Hero', though are not, of course, given with the kind of directness that opera demands.

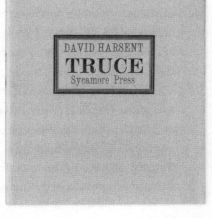

In a sense, of course, all poetry is garage-based. Whatever slant you put on that, Sycamore Press was a fine example of a fugitive tradition.

Alan Hollinghurst

Isherwood is at Santa Monica/The Well (1975)
A Florilegium for John Florio (1981)
Confidential Chats with Boys (1982)

I first met John Fuller when I came up to Magdalen College for an interview in December 1971; I was nervous and tongue-tied but I got in, and John was my tutor throughout my first year at Oxford, and occasionally thereafter. At the end of my very first tutorial he sold me a copy of *Nemo's Almanac*, of which he had taken over the editorship not long before, and I became hooked on it. Academically rather lazy, I seem to have worked very hard at tracing the quotations; I see I came seventh that first year, two places behind Helen Gardner and one behind John Carey, and over the following years crept up to fourth, just short of a prize. Certain quotations from *Nemo* bring back the atmosphere of my student years as vividly as anything, and the appearance of the new number each autumn was as exciting as Christmas is to a child. (In 1988, I took over from John as editor, when it ceased to be published by the Sycamore Press. To me it felt better than winning a prize; though I came to find that being Father Christmas was tiring work, and only stuck it out for nine years, as against John's ever-inventive sixteen.)

I had written quantities of poetry throughout my adolescence, and as an undergraduate went to the meetings of the John Florio Society, of which John was the senior member. All poems were submitted anonymously, though there was never any doubt as to the authorship of the ones John himself generously mixed in with our student efforts. My poems 'Isherwood is at Santa Monica' and 'The Well' were read at the Florio, and made up my very first publication as a Sycamore Broadsheet in 1975. The Isherwood poem was based on a TV documentary I had recently seen, though it may have given the fraudulent impression that I'd actually met him. At the time I was beginning to think about my graduate thesis on gay novelists, and he was a fascinating figure to me. 'The Well' comes out of my own Cotswold background, and clearly draws on a related interest in sexual mysteries. John said quite rightly at the Florio that we didn't need to be told the well was like a vulva, a thing of which I can anyway have had only a hazy idea; but he didn't insist on my changing it. He later passed on to me some high praise of the poem from William Empson, which I was thrilled by without fully believing it.

The poems of mine in *A Florilegium for John Florio* were written during the long dilatory period when I was a graduate student, and doing bits of teaching for which I felt anxiously ill-equipped. 'Rain' seems to express the melancholy and yearning of those years. 'The Derelict Houses at Great Barrington' is another Cotswold poem and my only attempt at writing in syllabics. I can't remember if I typeset it myself, but the exotic 'unknown grass' in line 9 should simply be 'unmown'. Again the poem evokes a relationship with an unnamed 'you', perhaps an imaginary lover, the pursuit of whom was soon to lead me off into the more specific world of the novel.

I suspect the best thing about *Confidential Chats with Boys* is its title, which I lifted from a book lent to my parents by a well-meaning aunt. It was by one William Howard MD, published in 1928; some of its violent and paranoid advice about how to identify and deal with homosexuals is quoted verbatim in the first section of the poem. The other four sections are more or less autobiographical; the last one describes listening to Shostakovich's death-haunted Fourteenth Symphony while eating a box of liqueur chocolates, both things done rather furtively. I do remember setting the type for this poem ('aud' for 'and' in part one is my error); and John's pleasure in finding the oddly phallic printer's flower that adorns the cover. This was my first (and so far last) pamphlet, and it makes me see how John's encouragement was essential to the years in which I was trying to be a poet: he read and commented on almost everything I wrote and by publishing some of it made my name known to a few interested readers, while opening up in me a sense of the possibility of becoming a writer.

Alan Hollinghurst

Isherwood is at
Santa Monica

Sycamore Broadsheet 22

Glyn Hughes

Almost-Love Poems (1968)

An early, perhaps the first, job that John Fuller had was as a lecturer at Manchester University. I lived near Manchester, and as a late starter in my career I knew one or two Manchester poets, principally Tony Connor. Tony was on the committee of the grandly named Manchester Institute of Contemporary Arts. I can't remember now whether it was Tony's or John's initiative, soon after he was invited onto the committee, to get MICA to publish a poetry-pamphlet series, but my first collection of poems was in that series edited by John Fuller, so he was in essence my first editor. He helped me a good deal with the poems that eventually became my first book with a major house — *Neighbours*, which was published by Macmillan — so I am grateful to him. He was sophisticated, which charmed me, and I think he regarded me as an ingenue, straight off the Pennine hills nearby.

The MICA pamphlet was only five small pages, entitled *The Stanedge Bull*, but remarkably it was reviewed warmly in the *Times Literary Supplement* and elsewhere, so it was a very good launch ... and is selling now through the usual traders for quite a sum. I met John a number of times then, visited him at his home in South Manchester, and so on. He was back in Oxford when the Sycamore Press broadsheets came out. It is no more than a single sheet of A4, the kind of thing I do regularly on my simple computer at home these days, but it was quite an enterprising *printing* and *publishing* exercise in those days, and I was very warmed by its appearance.

Philip Larkin

Femmes Damnées (1978)

12th June, 1978

Dear John (if you will allow me),

Many thanks for the 25 damned women. It looks very well, and my opinion of my early talents revives somewhat. A pity I didn't go on writing like this, instead of getting tangled up with Yeats!

Yes, of course, it was based on Baudelaire's *Femmes Damnées*, and I rather suspect that some of verse five may be a translation. It certainly doesn't sound like me.

The University of Hull   The Brynmor Jones Library

Librarian: P. A. Larkin, C.B.E., M.A., D.Lit., D.Litt., F.R.S.L.

J. Fuller, Esq.,   12th June, 1978.
4, Benson Place,
OXFORD.

Dear John (if you will allow me),

Many thanks for the 25 damned women. It looks very well, and my opinion of my early talents revives somewhat. A pity I didn't go on writing like this, instead of getting tangled up with Yeats!

Yes, of course, it was based on Baudelaire's Femmes Damnées, and I rather suspect that some of verse five may be a translation. It certainly doesn't sound like me.

I should be interested to know how it sells, and to hear any comments that may be made on it.

Yours sincerely,

Philip

Postcode: HU6 7RX   *Telephone:* 0482 46311   *Telex:* UNILIB HULL

I should be interested to know how it sells, and to hear any comments that may be made on it.

Yours sincerely,
Philip

Edward Larrissy

Three Poems (1977)

I first encountered John Fuller as a student, when I attended his lectures on W.H. Auden. These excellent lectures, as well as his own poetic practice, encouraged me to think of him as somebody who would not be constrained by what I saw as the rather limited range of effects possible in mainstream British poetry in those days. In 1975, I entered the *Isis* poetry competition, knowing that he would be the person chiefly involved in the judging: he was to select the short-listed eight poems, and Robert Lowell was to choose the winner from these. In the event, Lowell was hospitalised and Jon Stallworthy took over at the last minute. I made it into the final eight, though it was Mark Abley who won, with three of his poems making it into the final eight. Abley, a Canadian, has continued to write and publish good poems. My own entry, 'Four Ways of Reading Locke', had four different styles for each of its ways of reading, and these different points of view were supposed to reproach the narrowness of Locke's concept of understanding.

I still think that it is hard to imagine many other Oxford critics who would have promoted the claims of this poem. In any case, over the next couple of years I was writing poems which were influenced, I felt, by Frank O'Hara and John Ashbery, and I recalled my feeling that John Fuller would be quite likely to be open-minded about the effects of such an influence. I sent him three poems, and they were accepted surprisingly quickly, appearing as *Three Poems* exactly thirty years ago.

David Lehman

Breakfast (1968)

John Fuller published a broadsheet with five poems of mine under the title *Breakfast* in 1968. It meant a great deal to me as I had just turned twenty. I was spending the summer in an American academic programme situated at St Hilda's College in Oxford; Oxbridge dons (such as Fuller, John Carey and Alastair Fowler) taught classes or gave lectures, and we received college credit at our home institutions.

When John Fuller found out that I wrote poetry and had had some success in getting it published, he arranged for the two of us to give a poetry reading together. The broadside idea followed from that. To this day I feel indebted to him for this early recognition. His support and encouragement were invaluable.

As I recall, the very first broadside in the Sycamore series — named after the lane where John and his wife Prue lived — was devoted to a poem by John's father, Roy. I believe that *Breakfast* was the second in the series, which later included James Fenton, winner of the Newdigate Prize, and the Cambridge-educated Norman Bryson, who went on to a distinguished academic career.

John printed the broadsides on an old letter-press in his garage or basement. For *Breakfast* he chose blue lettering on ivory paper. It was a most handsome production.

I happen to be a great admirer of John's poetry and his critical work on W.H. Auden, and I feel that his writing has not been sufficiently recognized on this side of the pond. John is a poet of exquisite wit and formal artistry, with a subtle comic sensibility. I recall his being able to toss off a crown of sonnets — entitled, if I'm not mistaken, *The Labours of Hercules* — with nonchalance.

So pleasurable was the summer of 1968 for me that I chose to spend the following summer in Oxford as well. John let me stay in his house as a guest for a few nights and then he helped me locate a flat in Jericho. (It was the house at 5 Combe Road.)

For some reason I remember John's saying that he felt Arletty, in *Les Enfants du Paradis*, was overrated — or that at any rate he was immune to her charms. Why this particular remark made a lasting impression on me, I can't say. I was also grateful to John for introducing me to Philip Larkin's poetry, which I resisted initially and which I came to esteem greatly.

Harold Massingham

Creation (1968)

I've been a fan of Cynewulf, Caedmon, Aldhelm (and, apparently, a Saxon poet called Lul) since I met these guys in 1951. What stirred me were their poetic effects within the natural limitations of their pure Saxon tongue. Pure languages lead to thin lexicons.

My first sallies into their rugged world were versions of 'The Seafarer' and 'The Wanderer', both of which I included in my first book, *Black Bull Guarding Apples* (1965). I became increasingly involved, feeling that I was host to an avatar, not of a deity but of a poet called Cynewulf; and translating with a verve that Ted Hughes regarded as my 'true affinity'. As a result, my second book (*Frost-Gods*, 1971) contained versions of 'The Battle of Brunanburh', 'The Dream of the Rood', 'The Ruin' and thirteen

'Riddles'. The last included 'Creation', which I sent to John Fuller when he solicited a poem for the Sycamore Press.

In a later book (*Sonatas & Dreams*) I included versions of 'Iceberg', 'Anchor' and 'Sea-storm' in sequence as a three-movement sonata; and also 'Doomsday', based on parts of the Anglo-Saxon *Christ*. I am now struggling with a version of that wondrous Saxon poem 'The Phoenix'. I may get there if the muse pushes.

Needless to say, I was thrilled when John printed *Creation* way back in 1968.

Andrew McNeillie

Corncrake (1973), with Julian Bell (Illustrator)

I wrote that little poem on Inis Mór in the late spring of 1969. It was inspired by hearing the male corncrake's *crex crex crex crex* territorial call, up and down the island, and by reading riddles as discovered in Hamer's Faber anthology of Anglo-Saxon poetry. If I remember right, Julian Bell went and looked at a stuffed corncrake somewhere, possibly in the Pitt Rivers, and drew his marvellous image 'from the death'. You'd have to check that with him. I later published the poem in a sequence of bird poems called 'Plato's Aviary' (*Nevermore*, 2000). It took its rightful place under the title 'Riddle' in Chapter 8, entitled *Crex Crex*, of my memoir *An Aran Keening* (2001). A digitized and adjusted version of Julian's image for the Sycamore postcard forms the logo for my own Clutag Press. Clutag began life issuing poetry leaflets, handset on the Arab printing press that had previously been Sycamore's workhorse. When I was a belated undergraduate at Magdalen I used once in a while go out to see the Arab perform its tricks in John's garage at Benson Place.

Roger Mitchell

Edges (1973)

During the academic year 1972–73 I had a leave of absence from the university where I taught in the USA, and spent it in Oxford so that my wife could pursue a graduate degree there. I spent my time going to various lectures, working in the Bodleian Library, babysitting my two daughters, and going to poetry readings in the region. Among the poets I heard read that year in Oxford were John Wain, Peter Levi and W.H. Auden at Balliol College. At some point that fall, a sign caught my eye on a bulletin board somewhere about a Sycamore Press run by John Fuller. John and his father Roy, whom I later interviewed by mail for a journal in the States, were poets whose work I knew and admired. My memory is not completely reliable over such a span of time, but I think I went to hear John read his poems at one point. At any rate, the sign about Sycamore Press emboldened me to submit my work to such a fine press, an English press, without letting them know I was, in fact, an *Auslander*. I deliberately picked poems that would not 'give me away'.

Silly, I realize, because when I finally met John, he was very cordial and supportive. He even mentioned my name to the people at Faber, to whom I sent a manuscript late that year. Nothing came of it, of course, but John's generosity and support have always meant as much to me as his poetry and his valuable criticism of Auden. The poems themselves, as it happened, were written while I was living in Milwaukee, Wisconsin, which, because it lies on the shore of a very large lake, helped call up images of times I'd spent at the seashore as a child.

John Mole

Something about Love (1972)

John Fuller published my broadsheet in 1972, the year before the publication of my first collection *The Love Horse*, in which the Sycamore poems appeared with acknowledgements. At the time I was grateful for John's support. I particularly remember him commenting that 'setting it slug by slug in the composing stick is the real test of a poem' and I was happy to have passed the test!

When, with Peter Scupham, I founded the Mandeville Press in 1975, I came to know exactly what he meant. Peter and I were taught the craft of letterpress printing by John Myatt of the Cellar Press in Hitchin, and under his eye (along with Roger Burford Mason, later to found the Dodman Press) we produced a series of Cellar Press poems, using Faber's *Ariel Poems* as a model. One of the Cellar Press items was John Fuller's *Hut Groups*, illustrated by Carola Scupham. After Peter and I had gone on to start Mandeville we approached John again, and in 1980 we published his *The January Divan* with illustrations by George Szirtes. I mention all this as an indication of how there was open and generous communication between the proprietors of small, cottage industry presses.

Andrew Motion

The Pleasure Steamers (1977)

For me, as for most poetry-writing undergraduates during my time at Oxford, John Fuller was a presiding genius. A remotely presiding genius, in my case. I was at University College and, although I had friends who were taught by him, I only met him properly when he agreed to supervise my graduate thesis, which was on the poetry of Edward Thomas. By this time, I was writing the poems that were eventually published in my first collection — and as our supervisions got under way, John invited me to submit something he might publish with the Sycamore Press. I felt honoured: I already owned several Sycamore pamphlets and broadsheets, and I admired the authors, as well as the hand-pressed, heartfelt look of the series.

Andrew Motion

The Pleasure Steamers

Sycamore Broadsheet 24

The poem I gave John was 'The Pleasure Steamers', a poem in three parts which I thought might suit the broadsheet format because it was the right length, and because its subject was the Salter's pleasure boats which worked the Thames during the summer season and in winter were moored close to where I lived by Folly Bridge. I eventually chose it to be the title poem of my book.

We didn't spend much time actually printing the thing together (not enough, anyway, to prevent me from noticing a typo which somehow added to the sincerity of the production, rather than marring it), but I did feel a new kind of excitement when I received my free copies. Knowing the poem had John's blessing gave me a valuable sort of confidence. The same sort of confidence he gave to many other aspiring poets who were fortunate enough to benefit from his kindness.

Bernard O'Donoghue

A Florilegium for John Florio (1981)
Noctes Floriosae (1983)
Razorblades and Pencils (1984)
A Floribundum (1991)

There are few things I feel so strongly positive about as Sycamore Press, and nobody to whom I feel as beholden as a writer as John Fuller.

John published my pamphlet *Razorblades and Pencils* in 1984. It was my first publication, apart from individual poems in a series of Sycamore pamphlets made by John for the Florio Society at Magdalen College, where I was John's medieval colleague. The process of production of these beautiful little books was a very extraordinary one, and the most remarkable instance of writerly solidarity and generosity I have ever come across. John and a team of students and friends set the texts in John's study, to the accompaniment of Milhaud or Billie Holliday (an end in itself); then John spent Saturday mornings, wearing an oily overall in his garage, printing the pages. There was nothing in it for him apart from love of the process and the wish to advance the writing of these friends and students. I am sure many people have said the same, but I would never have published a poem — or even written one seriously — if I hadn't had the great good fortune to meet John.

I have never published anything that gave me more pleasure or thrill than that first book. Apart from the inherent generosity of this process, John has extraordinary editorial gifts, evident at Florio meetings as well as in the printing process. He had two abiding aesthetic principles which were of huge benefit to his writers: he wanted poems to make sense (he made no other formal or thematic strictures), and he insisted that the writer's text presented for printing had absolute authority. It shouldn't be tinkered with in the process. This democratic axiom was enormously productive; it made writers take full responsibility for what they wrote. And of course John, as a hugely gifted formal poet and weaver of literary structures, really could have pulled rank. The fact that he didn't, and that he took less gifted writers wholly seriously — evident not least in his corrective criticisms at Florio meetings — made people take themselves seriously too. He brought the same critical insights to bear on the poems of first-year students as he did on Auden.

I could say a lot more in detail, but I think in summary that to have been published by Sycamore Press was the most productive launching pad a writer could have, young or old (I was thirty-eight in 1984!).

Elise Paschen

Noctes Floriosae (1983)
Houses: Coasts (1985)

I had admired the poetry and the critical work of John Fuller and, when I arrived at Magdalen College in the autumn of 1982, I looked forward to studying with him. At Magdalen, I soon discovered that John Fuller also was the publisher of the Sycamore Press, and that he had published chapbooks of some of my favorite poets, including James Fenton and Andrew Motion. Sycamore Press had just produced Mick Imlah's *The Zoologist's Bath and Other Adventures*, a poetry collection which made an impact on us all.

During that first year of my M.Phil. course, I studied the poetry of W.H. Auden with John, and once a week we would meet in his rooms at the New Building to discuss Auden's work. At that time

John invited me to join the Florio Society, a group of Magdalen writers who gathered together to discuss each other's poems. If anyone became too self-congratulatory, Bernard O'Donoghue, a Florio Society member, would tease 'More power to your elbow.' John urged us to work on our poems, and at Magdalen College he created a close-knit community of poets and poetry lovers.

In the spring of 1983 John encouraged Mick Imlah, Nicholas Jenkins, Nicola Richards and me to launch the literary magazine *Oxford Poetry*. Since that time, he has navigated the journal through a succession of editors. When we served as co-editors, John showed us how to edit a magazine, even driving us around London, to help distribute the journals to book stores around the city.

Some time in 1984 (I had completed my M.Phil. degree and had begun writing a D. Phil. dissertation on W.B. Yeats's manuscripts), John offered to publish my work with Sycamore Press. Some of the poems he selected, such as 'Oklahoma Home' and 'The Front Room', were ones I had written as an undergraduate at Harvard. John also included new work, such as 'On a Plane Flying Down the Coast of Florida' and 'Bluebells'. Although he was less inclined to critique individual poems, John organized the arrangement of the manuscript.

I was drawn toward the title *Landfall* for the chapbook, but a poetry book by that name had just been published in America, so we chose a new name. John pointed out there were many images of houses in the poems as well as poems containing sea imagery. He suggested the title *Houses: Coasts*. We spent some time discussing the punctuation (*Houses, Coasts*, for instance), but then made the daring decision to use a colon. We also deliberated about the colors for the cover. The combination of sky blue and chocolate brown remains a favorite. We decided to use art work by David Kuhn, a college friend, who had created engravings originally inspired by Seamus Heaney's 'Bog' poems. Nick Jenkins wrote the biographical copy for the pamphlet, and Nick and John typeset *Houses: Coasts*.

During my five years at Magdalen, we spent many Saturday afternoons at John and Prue's house on Benson Place, working on various Sycamore Press pamphlets. I learned how to hand-set type. John sewed the binding for the chapbook covers. John and Nick, during typesetting breaks, would play chess. John also is a remarkable cook. He and Prue created delectable lunches — a smorgasbord of delicacies — from different exotic cuisines. I sampled my first Manhattan there! Their garden seemed tropical, blooming with various plants and flowers, and their cat, whose name I've forgotten, was an indomitable presence. Throughout the years various poets would help at the Press, including Bernard O'Donoghue and Mark Wormald, as well as Emily, John and Prue's youngest daughter.

John was an incredible mentor and editor. He championed and supported our poetry — from encouraging us to write new poems for the Florio Society to editing and publishing our work. He was brilliant and funny, generous and kind. I was honored to be counted among the poets John selected and privileged to be included in his company.

Peter Porter

Words without Music (1968)

42 Cleveland Square,
London, W2.,
September 20th., 1968.

Dear John,

   Here is the three-part poem I said I'd send as a candidate for selection for your printing press. It's sufficiently odd to require a bit of explanation. It starts serious and gets frivolous as it goes on. Each piece is musical in the sense that it is built on or influenced by ideas analogous to certain musical procedures. The first, which is a heavy Vietnam poem, has the four words of the title spread out in each stanza. I appreciate that this bears only the most superficial resemblance to the *cantus firmus* of a Bach prelude, but all analogies with music will be very approximate whatever you do. The second is a short free-form piece like a Mendelssohn *chant sans paroles*, but since it is all words and no tune, I've just turned the title round. The third is, I hope, comic; sardonic, even. Like a rondo, the opening line (tune) comes back in each stanza in a progressively more distant place until it reaches the first line position again. The different contexts are equivalent to the key changes of a musical rondo. I don't mean these rather slender musical analogies to be pressed too hard; they were just guide lines and amusing restraints on me when I was writing the poem. And they will help justify the title. I know you won't hesitate to tell me if you think it's too poor to use. In the second poem I wrote a line which now seems an unconscious piece of Ian Hamilton — 'we sit in green and hear of nothing good'. See those recent cryptic short verses of his in the *New Statesman*.

Best wishes,
Peter

42 Cleveland Square,
London, W.2.,
September 20th., 1968.

Dear John,

Here is the three-part poem I said I'd send as a candidate
for selection for your printing press. It's sufficiently odd to require
a bit of explanation. It starts serious and gets frivolous as it goes
on. Each piece is musical in the sense that it is built on or influenced
by ideas analagous to certain musical procedures. The first, which is
a heavy Vietnam poem, has the four words of the title spread out in
each stanza. I appreciate that this bears only the most superficial
resemblance to the cantus firmus of a Bach prelude, but all analogies
with music will be very approximate whatever you do. The second is
a short free-form piece like a Mendelssohn chant sans paroles, but since
it is all words and no tune, I've just turned the title round. The third
is, I hope, comic; sardonic, even. Like a rondo, the opening line (tune)
comes back in each stanza in a progressively more distant place until
it reaches the first line position again. The different contexts are
equivalent to the key changes of a musical rondo. I don't mean these
rather slender musical analogies to be pressed too hard; they were just
guide lines and amusing restraints to me when I was writing the poem.
And they will help justify the title. I know you won't hesitate
to tell me if you think it's too poor to use. In the second poem I
wrote a line which now seems an unconscious piece of Ian Hamilton -
'we sit in green and hear of nothing good'. See those recent cryptic
short verses of his in the New Statesman.

Best wishes,

Peter

Nancy K. Sandars

Idling On (1972)

In 1968 I was working as an archeologist overseas, mostly in
Greece, but I was in touch with the Fullers and going to Benson
Place when I was at home not far off in Little Tew. My memories
of John and Prue go back much further. Benson Place was where

one met exciting people, ate delicious food and smelled huge red roses. For me the thought of a printed poem was far beyond my dreams, though I had been writing poetry of a sort since I was a child and had been encouraged by Prue's mother and father, Cicely and Christopher Martin.

Prue now tells me that I and my sister Betty had a minor role in the beginning of the Sycamore Press. At the time, she was waiting for the birth of Emily, their youngest, so had some enforced idleness, and we gave her a book on typefaces which delighted and intrigued them both and put new life into the idea of a press in the garage by the great sycamore tree.

I loved the poems they published and was startled and delighted when in 1972 they suggested I should put something forward. I think I probably offered one or two, and I was very glad that they chose to have 'Idling On', which I had written one summer at home a little earlier. It attempts to catch some things half-remembered, another world, the brink of understanding, something that had once been understood and now lost, a dream that brought back a beginning almost before the beginning. The garden was always full of birds, one was so near to understanding but never quite got it full and true.

John and Prue know the garden well too; it still exists, though more dream than reality now.

Michael Schmidt

One Eye Mirror Cold (1970)

My recollections of dealing with Sycamore Press are blurry and sparse. I was never really part of the Sycamore group though I did admire some of those who were and I loved the Sycamore broadsheets.

I remember John's house in a quiet part of North Oxford — was it Benson Place, near Bardwell Road where I lived? It was, I seem to recall, modern at the time and comfortable in feeling, with family — two lovely little girls, perhaps? — and I think I remember Mrs Fuller being gracious and unfussed. I think I do remember a cumbersome old printing press, though it's hard to place where it was — a garage maybe? If I recollect, John, whom I did not know well (he was close to the Magdalen and Merton people, while I was in dowdy Wadham under the tutelage of the infant Eagleton) made some suggestions for improving the poems. I don't have a copy of the three-fold publication (it must have been my first 'separate publication'). I can't remember what was in it except a poem about a Mexican woman with a blank eye ('one eye mirror-cold, and one, Castilian blue'). I think the title came from that. I wish I could check. Perhaps somewhere a copy survives in an archive.

The other publications were, many of them, wonderful. The one I liked best, which I believe I still have because the poet means a lot to me, is *Our Western Furniture*. I certainly *hope* I have it.

John Fuller did important work with Sycamore. He was always discriminating, so it was a real achievement to be taken on and published by him, in company of other new and also some established poets. Sycamore had a feeling of conviction, which I associate with the smaller presses. Carcanet was just being born at the time.

I only visited John's house on one occasion. More frequently I saw him in his rooms at Magdalen. We have corresponded since, in particular about the novels, life and poetry of Roy Fuller, and I value his recent poems very highly.

Mark Wormald

Stills and Reflections (1988)
A Floribundum (1991)

When my maternal grandfather died in 1987, his extended family was not surprised by the specificity of the terms of his will. His one surviving daughter, my aunt, nevertheless found it an understandably tough task to execute his choice of bequests for his grandchildren. The fastidiousness with which now, from the grave, this wealthy youngest son and heir to the family firm matched this much-loved camera or viewfinder or flashgun with that grandson echoed the care with which, in his last years, he had made sure that neither of his two girls were themselves to benefit except from the residue of his estate, and made sure that they knew it. He had also done his best to ensure that none of the next generation would come into a penny until they had established their own financial independence. I don't think I knew, then, as an undergraduate at Oxford, taking a detour home at the end of my fourth term at Magdalen to pay a call on Hilda at Grandpa's bungalow in Solihull, quite how directly my mother's prolonged attempts to wrestle his intentions into a simpler and more humane form had hastened her own death, at forty-nine. Nor had I yet seen the letter that Grandpa had made a point of showing Hilda a year or two previously, in which her mother's sister sympathised at the evident disappointment at the birth of a second girl. But I did see the bewilderment and pain and maybe the fear in her eyes, which I mistook then for a daughter's grief, as she explained that, rather oddly, Grandpa had not put any one piece by for me, the youngest of Gwen's four sons. Instead, I could make my own choice from any of his belongings.

I left that day with my old Volkswagen hatchback crammed with two of Grandpa's favourite chairs. I still have both in my study. On the day, I was amazed and grateful for Hilda's generosity. I take it as typical of my widower father's Yorkshire upbringing, and of his own natural jaundice, that he should have reacted, when I reached home, by interpreting his sister-in-law's largesse as relief that I had not opted for the Jaguar, or the bungalow. I thought he was wrong, though, because of the other gift that Hilda threw in, with real tenderness — a large box of images, mostly of Gwen, from infancy to graduation day, that my grandfather had used his cameras to capture over the years, and which I discovered had been filed with the pictures of my own childhood, up to my mother's sudden death by heart attack when I was nine. There were newspaper cuttings of dinghy regattas and trophies won, and from my mother's own cremation and memorial service. And there was a round pewter framed convex mirror, which Mum had made for her parents at high school.

I sifted this trove over that Christmas, and then brought it back with me to College, where I shared it with Sarah Dence, then my co-editor at *Oxford Poetry*, and saw the photographs through her eyes. Learning to live with them, and indeed with any images of my mother since her death — neither my father nor my three older brothers found it easy or indeed possible at all to confront our loss except through getting on, and I had all but forgotten what she looked like — occupied my imagination fully enough for the first few weeks of term. Then, as if this were an inevitable and routine part of his duties as my tutor, John Fuller drew my attention to the theme of that year's Newdigate Poetry Prize: 'Elegy'.

The poems came quickly, and without any of that self-consciousness that often attended the writing of pieces for meetings of the Florio Society. For that purpose, extraordinary nerve was required, as an undergraduate, to submit a poem, nearly always in response to a theme, that would need to survive the photocopying and convenor's first reading before the meeting, and then the company of John, Bernard O'Donoghue, David Norbrook, Mick Imlah, Nick Jenkins, Frank Romany, Karen Leeder, Christiania Whitehead, John Mackinnon, Elise Paschen, Jane Griffiths: all of them kind but also resolutely honest. Anonymity was a prized principle, and a necessary one, as fundamental to the requirement that only those who had submitted a poem could attend; but submitting did also mean that one's poem had to take its chance of being read too late in a liberally oiled evening to get a reading as sober as one always hoped. And there were two more related risks, in these years when the first generation of green-screened Amstrads and IBMs were jostling for status with the older trusty typewriter. The first was that one's choice of font or format (I had a weakness for centring lines that inevitably found itself into the Newdigate poems) would allow readers to lift the veil before the end of the reading, which tended to inhibit the kind of criticism people felt comfortable offering. The second, initially much scarier variant on the first, was that people would guess wrong, but with unshakeable confidence; to which the only response was to learn boldly to criticise one's own work, to pretend that one didn't really understand or wasn't really convinced by a particular rhyme. In that low-lit circle, either of the alternatives, both of which in time I tried — braving it out in silence by burying one's face in a glass of red that was never deep enough, or nipping out to the bathroom, which meant a long trip up a cold New Building's staircase to the loos in the attic, or a dash out and along the colonnades to the most glamorous and draughty bathroom-cum-laundry in Oxford, the single-storey extension onto the deer park — lost their appeal.

There were, of course, compensations, and not just the poems we got to know and test so well, the vivid sense I have carried with me ever since that poets could and should be critics, that critics should if at all possible be poets. John and the Florio gave me the best single memory I have of Oxford. I think it must have been the Michaelmas term before my visit to Solihull that someone, I think it was Sarah, proposed a Florio pot-luck supper, which we would hold in the dining room in Magdalen Cloisters. John, delighted with the idea, promptly transformed it, not just by insisting on gastronomic cooperation — nothing would in fact be left to chance, or go to pot — but by enlisting a group of us to set not just the table but the menu itself, complete with appropriate quotations as *amuse-bouches*. That was our introduction to the cabinet in the study at Benson Place, with its drawers full of type. We had, I remember, to take apart, undo — distribute, he told us — a recently set page of poetry for the purpose. And in due course we also saw the secrets of John's garage, the old press with its sewing-machine treadle and the sewing it led to, the trick with the thread and the knot that took so long to master, like natural rhyme, in binding paper to board cover. The dinner was in due course terrific, apart from a nasty incident in the car en route from one of our flats off the Woodstock Road into College, when a pot full of goulash scalded my passenger's thighs. But it was the menu itself that lasted.

Writing the poems that became *Stills and Reflections* the next term, Hilary 1988, was by comparison quiet and low-key work. In part it was the thought of writing them for myself this time, in part because I knew, however unforgiving the eyes of the Newdigate judges might be, that their reading would happen at a safe distance from me, without all the intimate attention of a Florio night. But I must have absorbed the discipline that my two years of writing for sceptical but supportive Florio peers had given me; and just relaxed into the rhythms of grief and of the discovery that it opened onto, thirteen years after I had lost my mother. Without showing any member of the Florio circle but Sarah, I posted off my entry, my 'Elegy', under the title of 'Stills and Reflections', and forgot about it completely, until — I think it must have been early in the Trinity Term — I found a card from David Norbrook in my pigeonhole telling me that 'a poem with a distinctly Wormaldian feel has won the Newdigate'. I went straight to tell John, who beamed.

Two surprises followed. First, and for the only time in my life, I became a celebrity. Reading one of the poems, about my mother's convex pewter-rimmed mirror, at Encaenia, in subfusc, to a Sheldonian audience reeling from about an hour of University Latin, was one of life's odder experiences, but was as nothing to the shock of being recognized and greeted for about a week afterwards in the street by members of the congregation grateful to understand a word or two of what was being said.

Second, John asked whether I would be interested in publishing my poems with the Sycamore Press. I was flabbergasted. I had of course seen *Razorblades and Pencils*, and *Houses: Coasts*, and *Confidential Chats with Boys*, and had even associated their discreet, distinguished, timelessly spare look with the friends, and friends of friends, and mentors I knew had written them, quite recently — but still the thought daunted me, in general and in particular. I even began to regret having written so fluently: the prospect of setting line after rhyming line so painstakingly, with so many spacers, under John's tutelary eye, was daunting. So was the thought — and it was to happen years later, when a Seatonian Prize-winning poem I made the mistake of showing John elicited the response that, whatever its other merits, it certainly wasn't the sestina I had foolishly thought it to be — that the publisher would suggest changes.

In the event, it proved unusually, and in the history of the Sycamore Press I believe unprecedentedly, painless. Sarah Dence and I had by then become engaged, and were about to move into a Magdalen flat just round the corner from John and Prue, in Norham Gardens. That would have made the setting a bit handier, but it became unnecessary, for me at least. As I began my D.Phil. that October, Sarah found a job with *Daily Information*, the news and listing A2 broadsheet that a woollier John published from a house in Warneford Road. She soon became a dab hand with the phototypesetters in her first-floor office, with the darkroom under the stairs, and with the loom-like press down the garden in the shed. And so, one weekend in the late autumn of 1988, under the nose of John Rose and with the acquiescence of a still, I suspect, slightly sceptical John Fuller, who did nevertheless refrain from requesting changes to the poems, the pages were printed. A little later, the covers, some burgundy, some green, rolled off the press in the garage at Benson Place, complete with a print of a design done by Sarah's younger sister Rebecca of my mother's mirror, which still hangs, as I predicted it would, over our dining table, albeit now in the fens, and in which, 'marginal, like Auden's Breughel's Icarus', I still sometimes remember, and mourn my loss, as I enter the decade which became her last.

John, Sarah and I joined forces for a longish afternoon in December to fold pages, ensuring that the creases were as they should be with John's fine bone paddles (I confess I forget their proper name), and to stitch. And then it was done. '*First published at Christmas 1988 by the Sycamore Press, 4 Benson Place, Oxford. Text machine-set. Cover printed and sewn by hand at the press.*'

A conversation with
John Fuller

I met with John Fuller on 31 March 2007, at his home in Oxford.
Over the course of several hours, John discussed his work with
the Sycamore Press. Our meeting was not intended to serve as a
formal interview, but rather a casual discussion of his work. The
bulk of our conversation took place with a copy of the Sycamore
Press ledger accounting book in our hands and a draft copy of
the descriptive bibliography by our sides. In July 2007, I sent
John additional questions for his consideration, and his responses
have been incorporated in this text.

RYAN ROBERTS   Where did the name 'Sycamore Press'
originate?

JOHN FULLER   There is a very large sycamore hanging over
the garden. It drops leaves, keys and gum into the garden at
various times of the year and generally makes its presence felt.
It also contains beautiful owls and woodpeckers and doves,
making morning and evening sounds. So it was an appropriate
symbol for the pains and beauties of printing.

ROBERTS   Did you have any training or experience in
publishing prior to setting up the press?

FULLER   As a probationer B.Litt. student at Oxford you had to set up and print a poem from an Elizabethan manuscript, so I'd had some hands-on experience of type in 1960. I had also in 1958 been an editor of the university magazine *Isis,* which at that time had its office in the printing shop of the Holywell Press in Alfred Street. I knew all about the editorial technicalities of imposition, typography, proofs, line-blocks, and so on.

ROBERTS   Is the order of the publications in the ledger book more or less the order they were issued?

FULLER   They would be the order in which we knew we were going to do something and wrote it down and started to do it. They may not be in the order in which they were finally finished. In fact, I can't really remember the ledger book well enough to know how much that would vary as you were looking forward. For example, James's pamphlet appears pretty early I imagine. It was one of the first things we did, but it took some time, so I don't know how many broadsheets we did while we were working on that. I think the date listed in the ledger would indicate that we had finished. I mean it's a question of interpreting the ledger and probably I'm no better at interpreting it now than you.

ROBERTS   So the finished date may relate to when complimentary copies were available or perhaps to a set publication date?

FULLER   When complimentary copies were ready, I would triumphantly have given him [James Fenton] his 25 on... [*searching the ledger*] on the 18th of November. In August... we must have worked quite quickly actually, I now think. It was imposed in quarto and gave us great headaches and there exists at least one copy — George MacBeth's copy, that we sent to him at the BBC — did I tell you this? He wrote back and said, 'Fascinating poem. Do send me one that's correctly made up. I'll keep the one I've got as a rarity.' It must have been folded wrongly so that the sonnets were in the wrong order. That's always a hazard, isn't it, with a complicated imposition. We never imposed in quarto thereafter. For the pamphlets we used A4 sheets in folio, so it was much simpler. Even so, you've got a lot of pages and you've got to work it all out, as you know. Anyway, we must have worked quite quickly, then, if I wrote down in early August that we'd obtained the paper. I presume that's the moment when we were starting to print. But I don't think that you can rely on that entirely. We may have started and I may have written it all down later. I mean, it seems rather quickly to have done it. On the other hand, it would have been during the long vacation, you see, so we would have had August and September to do it. If I was sending out publicity postcards in October, I must have been hopeful that it was nearly ready — as, indeed, in a month it nearly was. So there's a bit of detective work involved, and your guess is as good as mine. Sometimes pamphlets would hang around for a long time. We would have planned it, and it may be apparent from these dates how long a pamphlet might take. I mean, I think of some of them as being nearly a year.

ROBERTS   And was James involved with some of the typesetting or any of the other aspects of the press?

FULLER   Well, he was certainly around a lot. He must have done some. I can't imagine why he wouldn't have done. [*Laughs*] I think he found it all fun.

ROBERTS   And at some point there was a special bound edition of *On Western Furniture*?

FULLER   Yes. When I was putting all the papers together for the Bodleian to look at, I came across little notes from my wife Prue, which reminded me that she read everything that was submitted, or things that we were going to print, and had strong views about them, and we discussed everything. So I think I haven't been acknowledging her part — her proprietorial part — in the press as much as I should have done. Because we certainly described both of ourselves as the printers, the publishers, the proprietors of the press, or however you call it, and were so described in some descriptions in magazines like *The Private Library*. So I think her interest and work should be acknowledged. She did a bookbinding course at that time, out of interest, and used the materials of the place where she was taking the course. I can't remember where it was — probably up at what is now Oxford Brookes University, but which was then the Polytechnic, using their binding presses. She did special editions of the Bryson and the Fenton.

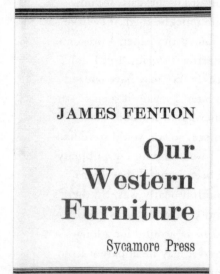

JAMES FENTON

Our Western Furniture

Sycamore Press

ROBERTS   So Prue bound a certain number of both Fenton and Bryson?

FULLER   Just a few... I can't remember how many. Again, it's Norman Bryson — maybe five or something? This is stirring my distant memories. In fact, we got to know of him through James [Fenton]. He was at Cambridge. And, did they go to school together? Anyway, Norman Bryson was kind of introduced to us through James, who liked his poetry and then, you know, we did as well and we published it. He became a rather distinguished art historian. He didn't remain a poet, Norman Bryson, but he's quite well known as an art historian. Whether aspects of the later biography of some of the writers [*laughing*], if they're not obviously known as poets, is of interest? But he was somebody who wrote poetry in his youth and not later on, which is perhaps of some interest.

Anyway, that was one of the things I was going to tell you — that in our previous conversations I perhaps hadn't been giving Prue her due as taking an interest in the press. And she would do a lot of printing, too. More in the early days than later, because she resumed her own teaching career as our girls grew up. She became very involved in special education in the 1970s. Our youngest child was born in 1968, so as she left infancy Prue took up more and more work. First with teaching the deaf and then with specialized sign systems for children with, you know, various forms of agnosia, aphasia,

NORMAN BRYSON

The
Swimmer
&
Other
Poems

Sycamore Press

or learning difficulties and made a great career of that. So, in the early days, she played much more of a part in the press than not.

ROBERTS   I think I saw in the archive an exchange between you and Prue about a particular poem. There was a letter that someone had written you, and she had left you a note about it…

FULLER   Yes, this is how it would happen very often. I would leave things on her desk that had come, saying, 'What do you think of this?' And she would go read through it and make a little list of thoughts and then we'd discuss it. It was really a collaboration of judgement very often in the early days, so I'd like her to have some place in the account.

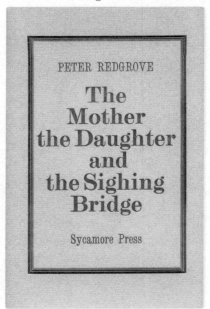

PETER REDGROVE

The Mother the Daughter and the Sighing Bridge

Sycamore Press

ROBERTS   So you did specially bound editions of Fenton and Bryson, but you also did a special edition of Peter Redgrove's *The Mother the Daughter and the Sighing Bridge*.

FULLER   We did different editions on better paper of some of the titles, so it is true that with the Redgrove poem *The Mother, the Daughter and the Sighing Bridge* we printed some copies on handmade paper that we put into marbled paper wrappers.

ROBERTS   And that was done up later than the ordinary edition?

FULLER   Yes — a lot later on. They must have been originally printed on the Hayle Mill paper. I had printed them on that perhaps not knowing what I was going to do with them. I hadn't realized it was so much later that we made up those special copies. Maybe I just intended to do it sometime, and the years went by.

I suspect the Redgrove is one of the things I didn't keep a copy of, which is very annoying. You will think me very careless about this, but it's one of those things that can happen. It was hand-marbled paper I bought at some sort of craft fair or something of that kind and it was wrapped around some card which was a sort of basis and then there was a label also printed on the same greyish paper.

The Hayle Mill paper was from a place in Kent somewhere where we ordered handmade paper for special purposes. And I think it's the place we also got the paper for the thing we did of my father's [Song Cycle from a Record Sleeve]. I think we had better look through everything and you just ask me the questions that overhang as we come to them.

ROBERTS   I believe there was a sample of the Redgrove text in the Sycamore archive, yes?

FULLER   Yes, I think there is. That was just the text. The cover would have been card with the title on the cover being a sort of narrow strip printed differently, so it wouldn't have looked like the cover of the ordinary edition. It would have been a little slip of Hayle Mill paper, which was sort of greyish blue, pasted on top of the marbled paper. This is not very useful to you, is it, scientific man? But is that clear enough if you want to describe it? I don't know why we don't have a copy left. As you can see we almost immediately sold all of them. I obviously intended to keep one back. It may well be that the text part in the archive would have been made up into a further copy and as time went by it never did. Maybe we ran out of marbled paper? Maybe I spoilt the last sheet or something. I really can't remember.

Some of these names in the ledger are familiar to me — G.R. Simms was a book dealer. He's also quite a successful detective writer and wrote books about the rare book trade as well.

I found the Hayle Mill paper difficult to print on. I think I hadn't got the art of damping. My impressions were always uneven. Somebody the other day was saying about something I printed, 'I love that special embossing effect that you got.' [*Laughs*] The ink was not biting properly, so I had to screw down the platen more than I should and of course that's the terrible thing that happened. I think it was one of the publicity cards… Anyway, should we go through everything just to let you be reminded to ask me questions like that when they crop up?

In your descriptions, do you simply repeat the same size each time for the broadsheets, or do you vary it if they seem to be different? Because I changed paper — the first set were on a sort of ordinary commercial but wove paper and then I moved to a smoother paper.

ROBERTS   Yes, I found there are some slight differences between them.

FULLER   Very slight, yes. Well that was carelessness and so forth, though they were still roughly, when finished, the same size, so they can stack together. But they're not identical.

Maybe that's part of their charm, who knows? [*Flips through the ledger book from beginning.*]

ROBERTS   One of the things I'm interested in, and I'm not sure how necessary it would be, is to describe in general terms the fonts used in all these various publications. It's of interest, and I'm very curious about it, but I'm not sure how reasonable it is to undertake such a thing for each item in the bibliography. After all, I assume in most of these that the fonts would be very similar, yes?

FULLER   I had very few fonts, and I just varied between two or three of them for everything I did. The main body type that we used was Modern 20 from Stephenson Blake and a larger font size of that in bold I used for the titling of pamphlets. The narrow type that I used for the words 'Sycamore Press' on pamphlet and broadsheet covers was called Consort Light Condensed. I forget the point size on that ... maybe 30? Is there a page in the ledger that describes this? Where we bought all the stuff in the beginning? [*flipping to front of ledger*] Here we are: 12 pt Consort, 48 pt Modern 20 Bold. How many different types do you think there are?

ROBERTS   I saw in a letter you made reference to Times New Roman, but I think there may only be a few variations.

FULLER   See, I did buy some other dusty cases of type, mostly Caslon, from a printer that was going bust, and on occasion I used that. I'm not so sure I didn't use some of that for the Peter Redgrove.
    The title page inside Redgrove's pamphlet — that is Caslon. And I didn't like it. I used it, including this rule, which I thought went rather well with it. And I didn't really like it. I don't know that I ever used it again. I may have done.

ROBERTS   And the 'Sycamore Press' lettering on the pamphlets?

FULLER   That's Consort Light Condensed. And I think that was 30 pt, so what that 12 pt Consort that we were looking at in the ledger meant, I don't know.

Anyway, I always ended up with bits [of pamphlets]. Some sheets I'd have too many of, so that I'd run out of them when making up copies. So there would be quite a few left over of one that I'd printed off too many. And I've got more covers of that poem of my father's than I had text for. [*Holds the cover in hand and points*] There's the 'embossed effect' [*said sardonically*] — very difficult to print that, because it would go pale in one corner. I reckoned it didn't matter for a cover, so I ground the type into the paper in order to get as good an impression as I could. Some people found this amateurishness rather fetching, but I was always ashamed of it.

It was always very difficult ... This brass rule comes in particular sections so you piece it together to make up any shape you like and then you screw it in with the wooden furniture and metal quoins, which you tighten up with a key. It joins up, and it should do exactly so you don't see the joins, but it was always very difficult to do so you didn't see the joins. And there you see a white line. You shouldn't really see that. Each line of the piece of brass rule printing the border should be beautifully and equally black. Though where some of these have joined, it's not too bad. These would have been shorter bits, you know, to make up the exact area that I wanted. And I can't remember how many there would have been. There — up in the right corner [*points*] — you can see they're not quite aligned properly. That's due to the way I've screwed in the furniture. It's very hard to do that. You might spend a long time measuring up, screwing it into the forme to get it right. And that little wiggle there is a mistake... though there it shows you that it's done by hand.

Here's one of the Brysons that was bound. But it's difficult to bind thin things, isn't it? I mean, you don't have a spine, so in some ways it's rather pointless. It may be that Prue only did a very few — might have only done two of them. [*Searches in ledger for Bryson entry*] No, it doesn't say, does it? I think she only did a very few, just for interest. Did I sell one of them? [*Searches*] No. 'Four hundred thirty copies' — that was quite a lot for us. And it was hard to sell. At one point I did a little wrapper with some quotes from reviews to entice people to buy it.

ROBERTS   And you printed the wrappers, as well?

FULLER   Yes. [*Turns pages in ledger book*] Ah, now hang on. Here's something on the 12 pt Consort. We used that for the Harsent pamphlet and also for Alastair Fowler. So, yes, we used that as the body type for certain things, but the broadsheets were all in Modern 20. Modern 20 is quite small, isn't it? So we had two sizes of Modern 20 — the smaller and the bold — and the body type. And we had two sizes of Consort — Consort Light Condensed and just Consort. I think that's what it is now. And then, you know, the occasional sports, like using a bit of old Caslon that showed up. It seems to be very worn. I think it had been very heavily used, this Caslon. I think it's a nice type in itself, but this version of it seemed a bit elusive somehow, seemed a bit vanishing...

ROBERTS   David Lehman, in his piece for the book, says that it was here in Oxford that he met you.

Our Western Furniture.		James Fenton.	200 copies + 10 bound.			
1968						
9 August	60	Cartridge paper for bound copies. (Daler A series) *amount decided is for total lot = circa 1100 sheets.*		—	11	—
"	900+	Blenheim wove 40 lb crown folio		2	13	3
11 oct	100	Postcards for publicity		—	2	—
30 oct		Type and art rule for cover		2	16	3
7 Nov		Cover paper		1	7	6
15 Nov		Cartridge paper for endpapers		—	8	6
16 Nov		Postage (9 @ 4½ + 1d for envelope)		—	3	9
29 Nov		Postage for publicity 20 & 4d		—	6	8
16 Dec		Postage		—	7	-
"		Postage		—	1	3
15 Feb		Postage		—	2	6
24 April		Postage (to date)				8
2 July		Charge for binding materials at the Tech.		—	12	-
		Ink		—	2	6
2 Jan 70		Postage			1	6
6 Jan 70		Postage			2	6

FULLER   He was in one of the classes that I taught for the Massachusetts summer school, which was, I think, at Trinity College over the summer. Students would come over to experience Oxford, and I took on some courses. He was bright and interested and must have shown me his poetry… and we printed it.

[*Turns to front of ledger*] Now, *Our Western Furniture…* seems a lot to say about it. We used linen thread for these pamphlets. It had to be specially purchased and it's very thin and very strong. I mean, it's obviously stronger than cotton. It does come in various thicknesses, and I had various hanks of it, as I had acquired some in the course of things that I found was distinctly thinner. So I ended up maybe using linen thread of different thicknesses at different times, maybe even for the same pamphlet … maybe ran out of the particular dyed colour that I'd got for that pamphlet and used some standard black that I'd dyed for general purposes. I used little dye capsules that you use for dying cloth.

ROBERTS   You published twelve copies of *Our Western Furniture* that Prue bound and that were all numbered and signed by James.

FULLER   Yes. I never knew whether to number and sign copies. I think I was somehow in revolt against the idea of creating a collector's item from the beginning. Although the print runs were rather small, I felt they ought in theory to be open-ended. So things did run out and that was just hard luck. You just had to judge the number in advance. But I didn't want to create immediate rarities. So that's why we didn't really number copies. We did on certain occasions.

Philip Larkin

As an initial effort, as I say, imposed in quarto with all these sonnets, *Our Western Furniture* was quite an effort and we were quite proud of it at the time, even though so many of the sonnets were rather grey in effect. Such fun to do.

Femmes Damnées

And we didn't have type with lines across the top. The Japanese name 'Ba-sho' should have a line over the 'o', I believe. And I don't know why I decided to hyphenate

Sycamore Broadsheet 27

it instead. It was probably some metrical effect as it were. It could have been 'Ba shō', but we didn't have a line above. For example, where we needed an acute accent on the 'e' of the title of Larkin's *Femmes Damnées*, what I did was to cut a piece of leading that goes between the lines of type, file away a slot above the letter in the slug of type, in the body of the slug of type, and insert it with glue just to the right height so that it printed as an acute accent. [*Laughs*] That was real Heath Robinson stuff, and I was quite pleased to have done that.

ROBERTS So Fenton's poem just coincided with your getting the press?

FULLER Yes. I mean, we didn't buy the press to do his poem. I think it was just a coincidence. I had encouraged him to go in for the Newdigate, and he'd read up about the opening of Japan and read lives of Commodore Perry and all that stuff. And he did it, and won it, and the two things just sort of came together. It seemed an appropriate thing to do. I think if it hadn't been so much on home territory, because he was then a very bright student who became a friend... and it seemed the obvious thing, to do it. I mean, if it had been by somebody else we might have said, 'No, it's too difficult. It's too complicated to print well. We can't do anything as elaborate as that.' But, I think we just said, 'What the heck. We'll do it.'

I think you might say, mind you, that the twelve copies are on a different paper, as well as being specially bound. They're on this cartridge paper. I think, if you look, it's on a thicker paper than the ordinary edition.

ROBERTS Your ledger states the ordinary edition was made up of 200 copies, but the publicity card for the book states 230 copies are available.

FULLER   Was it maybe that we intended to print 200 copies, and when we actually printed it off the waste was not as much as expected, or we continued further with the amount of paper we'd got? And by the time we were printing the postcard for publicity in October we actually had 230 copies to dispose of? That seems to be a likely explanation.

ROBERTS   So what determined, for the broadsheets, the number to be printed?

FULLER   I suppose we were influenced by the thought that with certain poets we could, in theory, sell a lot of copies. In other cases, I think we just went crazy when printing and there was more daylight than we thought and the paper was there and we just sort of went on for longer doing it. I think that was true of Bernard Bergonzi's. We had printed a vast number. I seem to remember that it was purely accidental — just a sort of burst of energy. Because when you're actually out there doing it — there's the paper, it's all inked up — you go on doing it as long as you can, until it gets dark. And you want to print them all in one day. So 200 copies is a fair number, but if it's all going well you can get through many more. The thing goes 'thwump, thwump, thwump', and if you're hand-feeding the paper in regularly and you don't have to keep stopping for disasters you can get many more done. I think on certain days we found ourselves printing more than we really should have done. I think that's the answer. It's pretty arbitrary, actually. It's to do with printing conditions and whether things have gone wrong or whether the daylight continued long enough for us to print. Not very serious reasons. How many did we do of Thom Gunn — 500? I must have thought, 'This is Thom Gunn. I can surely sell 500.'

ROBERTS   And so you had approached Gunn with a letter requesting a poem for the series?

FULLER   Yes, I must simply have done that. I think that's how I worked. I would try to think of whom I would like to publish and write to them. I mean, there were people I mooted it with, on and off, whom I never published. Some of whom there were no letters about in the archive. I mean, Seamus Heaney was someone I was thinking of doing. With Gunn, we had been in touch about something else. I may have asked Gunn for something for a series I was running in Manchester. I had just edited a series for the Manchester Institute of Contemporary Arts of poets. They did about six or seven little pamphlet collections which I chose and which were published by MICA. I think I may have tried to get him for that. I'd reviewed his reissue of *Fighting Terms* in Ian Hamilton's *The Review* and I think he wrote me a letter about that. That would have been in 1962 or 1963. So we were a bit in touch. I never met him, but as you can see in the archive it was a friendly correspondence.

ROBERTS   And Nancy Sandars...

FULLER   Nancy is a good friend of ours and a very good poet. She's since published a book of her poems. Actually, she's probably one of the oldest poets to publish a first book of poems that you could think of. She was in her eighties when she published it? It was she and her sister Betty who, instead of sending flowers when we had our youngest daughter and Prue was a-bed after the birth, they sent this book of type faces. Really the inspiration to go ahead with printing.

ROBERTS   And here we come to James Fenton's *Put Thou Thy Tears Into My Bottle*.

FULLER   This is the one I misprinted the title. He didn't seem to mind. I had some theological explanation for sticking with it, quite apart from the laziness in order to reprint the whole thing entirely, having done it. I think we could just draw a veil over that. No doubt if you don't say anything about it being an error it will become a sort of postmodernist twist on the biblical text by James himself whenever somebody writes up his work.

[*Turns to Anthony Furnivall's pamphlet*] And then our attempt to print music. He was, I think, an organ scholar at Magdalen. I can't remember exactly how I decided to print his song.

ROBERTS   So how did you go about setting the music for this?

FULLER   I used... you know that stuff, which in England is called Letraset, where you rub letters from a sheet? It's got a slightly sticky back and when you rub it like a transfer the letter comes off. You can get ordinary fonts and you can get a sheet with musical symbols. I got staved paper, Letraset

musical symbols, did a score and had a zinc-lined block made from it through a printer. I did the circular staves, by the way, with a pair of compasses. Quite tricky to do them neatly enough to reproduce, and then did the letters around. [*Checks ledger book*] There is an acute on Mallarmé, obviously, but I wouldn't have been able to do that on my type. I certainly wouldn't have done an accent on a little bit of type in the way that I described for the Larkin poem.

Furnivall just set this Mallarmé poem, and I was rather intrigued by the challenge of publishing music. It just seemed an interesting technical challenge. And it was, really, because normally music is quite big — you prop it up on the piano and look at it from a distance. That was the largest size I could do getting those blocks into my forme, which is quite small. I seem to remember that the blocks filled out the entire forme.

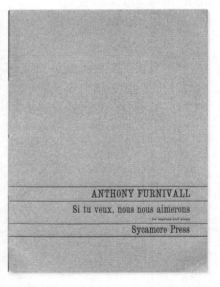

ANTHONY FURNIVALL
Si tu veux, nous nous aimerons
for soprano and piano
Sycamore Press

ROBERTS   And then there are the Nemos ... I'm considering separating them out from the rest of the bibliography, perhaps under a miscellaneous category.

FULLER   I think that in the sort of technical bibliographical sense it was just another of my activities that I brought under the umbrella of the press in order to help to market it. I think I thought I was simply going to account for it in the ledger as though I were publishing it, that I would include it for accounting purposes in case I was ever going to have to pay tax. In at least one instance, I ran out and photocopied some more. [*Consults ledger*] Yes, Truexpress — I must have taken my last copy along and had them do some sheets from it.

ROBERTS   So Standard Press would have done the original, but Truexpress would have handled the copies?

FULLER   Truexpress was just a little local print shop that would have given me something I could bind myself. I must have had a cover block made of the whole of the typographical cover of the Standard Press edition, just for convenience. And then I printed it on this yellow Glastonbury where I obviously had an awful lot of it as I'd used it often. So that was in 1973 that the press itself would have printed off the covers.

I think Nemo's presence in the ledger was just a sort of accounting thing. I sort of associated Nemo with the press, because I was doing the publicity postcards and it was something I was doing...

ROBERTS   There's another instance of your having a block made in the same way as in 1973.

FULLER   Did I do it twice? It had lurches of publicity. If it was mentioned in a national paper, which it sometimes was, there would be a surge of people interested in it and wanting extra copies. So there was quite a sizeable circulation at times. In looking at the ledger, I see that I obviously did the second impressions twice. So I don't know quite how you should deal with it. It maybe just needs a page in which all this is described somehow. In general it was included, as it was an activity of mine and it was, as it were, nominally published by Sycamore Press. I mean, it *was* published by the press. It had 'Sycamore Press' on the cover. I had forgotten how completely it was included in the ledger.

[*Looks at the entry for Nemo's Almanac,* 1973] Ah, Standard Press. Yes, I did shop out the printing. We moved between different places. But Truexpress was the place that would do the immediate offset reproduction for the purposes of the second impression, but the major item was from

Standard Press, which the previous editor had used. I started out with them and then moved somewhere else for some reason, so it was a jobbing. We could never have printed a *Nemo's Almanac* on the Arab press. It may be that originally I thought that we could, but it would have been quite a job

ROY FULLER

Song Cycle from a Record Sleeve

Sycamore Press

of printing. Even though the pages are sparse, it would have been a headache.

ROBERTS   The *Nemo* entries in the ledger were from the mid- to late 1970s, but you stop listing them even though you still printed promotional cards for later issues from the 1980s.

FULLER   I didn't do promotional cards after I gave up editorship, but why I stopped writing down the details in the ledger I've no idea. I certainly enjoyed publishing the publicity cards, because I would use little blocks that I'd acquired in one place or another and write copy to accompany the block.

ROBERTS   And now we move to Michael Schmidt's *One Eye Mirror Cold*.

FULLER   I was interested in seeing so much correspondence in the archive from Michael Schmidt and quite a lot about his setting up the Carcarnet Press. I think that was of some interest, particularly to the Bodleian, who are interested in acquiring the archive because they're interested in private printing associated with Oxford.

ROBERTS   And here for Fowler's *Seventeen* we have the larger font on the cover.

FULLER   Yes, on the cover we used wood lettering normally used for posters. I don't think there is any way of describing that. We inherited the font from one of these printing firms that was going out of business. There was quite a lot of that sort of thing. But we didn't often use it, because it was difficult to print from, difficult to get an impression. A lot of it is very large, typically used for newspapers.

MARK MEMBERS

Iron Aspidistra

Sycamore Press

ROBERTS   For Roy Fuller's *Song Cycle* you limited the printing to sixty?

FULLER   Yes. We did sixty copies because he was sixty in February 1972. Born in 1912.

ROBERTS   And there were around thirty extra copies printed...

FULLER   Yes, I suppose I couldn't bear merely to do sixty. So there were sixty signed and numbered and then some unnumbered copies. I don't know if that's a criminal thing to do from a publishing point of view, but...

We did a similar thing with a little pamphlet for Anthony Powell's birthday. Was that his seventieth birthday? For that, my father did a spoof of a poem by one of the characters from his novel, Mark Members. That was seventy copies, and I think we did extra then. It seemed a small number to produce absolutely.

ROBERTS   You published several pieces by your father. What was that experience like — the mixed roles of both publisher and son?

FULLER   The first broadsheet was by him — a rather powerful poem about the Cold War, which we were very glad to have. I'd always wanted to include him where appropriate in anything I edited. Reverse nepotism, perhaps. We had a fine and mutually encouraging relationship.

ROBERTS   Now the *Bestiary* was also signed and limited. It would have been printed elsewhere, yes? The ledger states you paid for 'block mounting'.

FULLER   I was going to print it, but it's very difficult to print linocuts. You can't really do it on an ordinary letterpress machine, because you can't get the rich area of black. Normally printing a linocut you'd be... well, an artist making linocuts really has to have a very heavy screw press and flat bed and so forth. We tried. I mean, we did some experiments. We tried and it was hopeless. We had some blocks made so that I could do it, and it didn't work. I had to have them mounted on type-high blocks for my machine, but it didn't work so we handed them over to the Oxonian Press, which is here in Oxford, and they did it by whatever means they would have employed there. There was some overprinting involved. I think it was an Indian fabric block that she had. She liked for some of them to have a bit of texture.

ROBERTS   And these were put into a plastic sleeve?

FULLER   Yes. I think Brigitte had her ideas of how it could be done. Yes, with a twisted gold thread that went through a punched hole at the end of the plastic envelope and then was held down by a sticker, a gold sticker. I remember doing all that and it was quite an elaborate thing to do one way or another. And I don't think all those cards came out the same size. Although it was done by the Oxonian Press, when they came to trim them they were not all absolutely uniform. At the time it was slightly irritating, but, there again, it doesn't matter in the long run.

ROBERTS   You later published the verse elsewhere, yes?

FULLER   Yes. I printed them in a book of children's poems. I would have ideally liked to keep them as they were, but they and other poems I was collecting in a volume that was produced by Salamander Press were illustrated anew by Nicholas Garland. And I really just had to accept that. It applied to another poem I published somewhere in some children's magazine, a poem called 'Geography Lesson', which is about the way the British Isles looks like a person who is holding Ireland on her lap and it's falling away, it's falling off her lap. And there was a political point made there. You know, pictorially the map looks like a person and you can describe features of the person in terms of the geographical features. It had been perfectly well illustrated, but it still got redone.

[*Turns to an entry for Sycamore Card no.* 1] Ah, the first of the cards… McNeillie now uses the image of the corncrake as the symbol of his Clutag Press. And on card number two I got

1.	P to K4	P to K4
2.	Kt to KB3	P to Q3
3.	P to Q4	B to Kt5?
4.	P takes P	B takes Kt
5.	Q takes B	P takes P
6.	B to QB4	Kt to KB3
7.	Q to QKt3	Q to K2
8.	Kt to QB3	P to QB3
9.	B to KKt5	P to QKt4?
10.	Kt takes KtP!	P takes Kt
11.	B takes P ch	QKt to Q2
12.	O-O-O	R to Q1
13.	R takes Kt	R takes R
14.	R to Q1	Q to K3
15.	B takes R ch	Kt takes B
16.	Q to Kt8 ch !!	Kt takes Q
17.	R to Q8	Mate

actual moveable chess type, which these days must seem a very cumbersome way of doing it, but presumably for chess problems in newspapers this is what you did. Each square, whether it was a black or white square, whatever piece it had on it of whatever colour, had a different piece of type. So you made up your 8 × 8 square, choosing whatever you needed to make up the position. That was great fun. I enjoyed ordering that stuff and doing it. Should have done more chess cards. Did you play this game over? Because it's an astounding thing to be playing in the theatre, and it's a wonderful queen sacrifice as I remember. It's an extraordinary game. I mean, the Duke of Brunswick was no good at all, so Morphy could really show off and give him all his pieces and then deliver mate in a casual way. Tremendous stuff.

ROBERTS   You have an entry in the ledger for a title by Ian Hamilton to be titled *In Dreams*.

FULLER   Yes. He was an old friend, and I was really wanting to do this seriously. As his poems were so short, I was proposing, rather like Alastair Fowler's *Seventeen*, a small format in which the poems wouldn't be followed by a great deal of space on the page after each one. And he obviously thought this was inelegant somehow. Dear Ian. And so, in a perfectly friendly way he said *not on your life* and it was published somewhere else. In fact, I think he did publish a pamphlet of that title... have you come across it? *In Dreams*? I can't remember if it was actually called that.

ROBERTS   There's *Pretending Not to Sleep* and *Returning*, but I don't remember anything titled *In Dreams*.

FULLER   I can't remember whether I made up a dummy to send him. I think perhaps I did, and he must have thought it was too ridiculously small. But I rather like the idea of tiny little things. John Cotton, of whom I did a broadsheet, was himself a small printer, and he used to do tremendously small things. Auden's first book is small in size. Stephen Spender printed it on a small press.

ROBERTS   Did I see in the archive that you gave a lecture about Auden's poem 'Sue'?

FULLER   Yes. I included in the archive a copy of the lecture I did which finishes with 'Sue' as an example of problems that are going to face an editor. It was a talk I gave to a group of sixth-form masters, and I gave it at the request of a colleague of mine who was a French tutor at the time and asked if I'd speak on some subject to them. And I thought they would be interested in this. How would an editor approach a definitive edition of Auden, who was always mucking about with his poems and leaving things unfinished and so on? And this was the problem of the reconstructed poem, which I think on the broadsheet itself gives you the effect of missing bits in plaster of a statue that you have to, as it were, imagine precisely what was there in the first place. It's as though you were giving arms and a gesture of the wrist to the Venus de Milo. And it was very much like that, you know — real guesses, because he just was scrawling it for himself in this notebook and it was a real headache.

ROBERTS   Where did you find the poem?

FULLER   I was sent photographs of the pages of the notebook by Edward Mendelson — the notebook at that stage still belonged to Christopher Isherwood — together with Isherwood's transcript with blanks and guesses, and I and Ed worked on the Isherwood version and supplied the missing bits, improved upon it, and put the stanzas in order and so on and made the best we could of it. So it's not a poem that can very easily be regarded as authentic or authorial or canonical. It was an interesting case, so I used it as an example in my lecture of how an editor goes about dealing with texts that are not quite there, as it were.

Because there are ordinary problems about which text to print if a significant revision has been made. Do you just simply end up printing both? These problems are part of the whole business of bibliography and textual criticism generally. What is the poem? You don't know quite what it is. It could be one of several things in the course of time, over time, particularly if the author is careless or meddling with his own work.

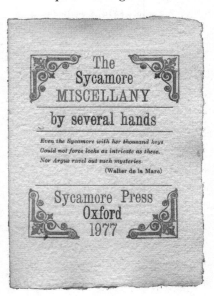

ROBERTS   For *The Sycamore Miscellany*, were you going to do this as a series?

FULLER   I was going to do little gatherings of eight pages each, which would be collected together and perhaps even eventually bound in such a way that it would have a little spine. That was the idea. It intrigued me to do that, and with paper that I made myself. Only I ran out of steam.

ROBERTS   And the *King of China* … you had different people contribute verses, yes?

FULLER   Yes. That was James's idea. He had a few verses and
we got other people to write them as well. Rather salacious
verses about this homosexual king of China. And various other
things were lined up, and I printed another sheet on both sides
— four more pages — and it needed more before that would be
a gathering that I would circulate, and I just sort of stopped,
I'm afraid. But the first did circulate.

Now, as for my *Bel and the Dragon*, I had to circulate
copies free of charge to heads
of houses and professors for
having won this sacred poem
prize. I mean, originally I
thought the proprietor of a
small press shouldn't publish
his own work, so I tried to
stick to that, but not always, so
I did this.

Printing white on the cover
was a risky thing — white ink
on dark background. Since
it was rather indistinct, some
Babylonian image or whatever
it was, that seemed to work
reasonably well. But it gave me some moments of anxiety.

ROBERTS   And you did three pamphlets for the John Florio
Society...

FULLER   It wasn't done officially for the society it was
sponsored by, really. It was just that we all got together to print
the poems, my having said that I'd be happy to supervise and
do most of the work. So it was a collaborative thing, but still
the Sycamore Press.

[James Fenton enters the room just as we come to the entry for his pamphlet *Dead Soldiers*.]

FULLER   James, you didn't help to set your *Dead Soldiers*, did you?

FENTON   No, no… You invented the cover for it. They were chess pieces?

FULLER   No, they were wooden blocks that pre-existed. I made a lot of use of small decorative wooden type blocks on all these things. There were things that looked like little fountains that I used on the Florio pamphlets, and others that were like playing card symbols. I think we bought type cases full of them from these firms, at least one firm, that was going bust. So there were some little line blocks with sort of rugby tackles and things like that, and there were these wooden things. And these were separate little shapes. I don't think they were meant, actually, to be chess pawns. I've seen them described like that and they certainly look like it, but they're a bit more elongated, aren't they, than a chess pawn would be. I don't know what they are, but they were pre-existing decorative wooden printing blocks that I just made use of. I mean, it's very appropriate to think of them as pawns.

Now, for *Capital Letters* I did have the text farmed out to a printer, who did it in Linotype to print it off myself. So I collected the metal type set in Linotype from the Oxonian Press, and then we machined it ourselves. It seemed to be cutting a corner, but it was a way of getting it done.

ROBERTS   What advice would you give to someone contemplating the purchase of a small printing press?

FULLER   Now that you have computerized desktop publishing, it would seem tremendously quaint to go in for letterpress on the small scale that we did. You'd have to be quite clear that you would be likely to enjoy oiling and freeing a seized-up cast-iron monster, cutting new leather strips for the runners that the ink-rollers run on, picking up the type that you drop on the floor, setting words letter by letter back to front and upside down, warming the ink, &c. If you just wanted to produce poetry pamphlets, there'd be better ways of doing it, surely. But some people like tending machines rather as they might like to keep horses. We certainly enjoyed it. It might be hard to get the equipment and type now, of course.

ROBERTS   When you think back on the Sycamore Press, what is the one image that most comes to mind?

FULLER   The smell of the rubber solution we used as a cleaner, candlelight as evening came on, a cup of coffee on the little wooden ledge attached to the press, and one icy foot pushing on the treadle.

Descriptive bibliography

Because the Sycamore Press did not issue multiple editions, and given the general uniformity of type throughout the press's published output (owing to the small number of fonts used by the press), specific font information is not provided for each individual item. As described by Fuller in the interview earlier in this volume, 'I had very few fonts, and I just varied between two or three of them for everything I did.'

ISCC–NBS Centroid Color Charts (SRM 2106) were used for colour identification of the paper bindings and any significant printed colours apparent within the works themselves. In cases where the exact shade, hue or colour was not absolutely essential to identification, less formal colour identification was employed. The initial lettering of text is black unless otherwise indicated. Where ink colours vary within a given specimen, the colours are identified in brackets preceding the affected text, and a return to black is likewise indicated in brackets.

Measurements of material are provided, usually in inches and millimetres, though in the case of lines or rules only millimetres are used. I caution to note that the nature of private press printing and guillotining of pages often results in the production of similar items of slightly different size. Such differences should not be an indication of varying editions or printings, but are rather the result of casual trimming on the part of the publisher.

Pamphlets

<table>
<tr><td>A1</td><td>James Fenton, Our Western Furniture
(November 1968)</td></tr>
<tr><td>FRONT COVER</td><td>[four lines of varying thickness the width of cover] | JAMES FENTON | [in vivid red (11)] Our | Western | Furniture | [in black] Sycamore Press | [four lines of varying thickness the width of cover]</td></tr>
<tr><td>TITLE PAGE</td><td>None.</td></tr>
<tr><td>IMPRINT PAGE</td><td>[on verso of front cover] First published 1968 | by the Sycamore Press | 4 Benson Place | Oxford</td></tr>
<tr><td>COLLATION</td><td>Nine sheets measuring 9¼ × 7¹⁄₁₆ in. [235 × 180 mm] folded at centre to 7¹⁄₁₆ × 4⅝ in. [180 × 117.5 mm]. Unnumbered. [1]: 'OUR | WESTERN | FURNITURE'. [2]: blank. [3]: 'To J. B. Keates'. [4]: blank. [5]: 'Part One: | Under the Tokugawa'. [6]: blank. [7–14]: text. [15]: 'Part Two: | 1854'. [16]: blank. [17–24]: text. [25]: 'Part Three: | Under Western Eyes'. [26]: blank. [27–33]: text. [34–36]: blank.</td></tr>
<tr><td>BACK COVER</td><td>[four lines of varying thickness the width of cover] | [text in vivid red (11); quote by Commodore Perry in his report to Congress in 1856] | [in black; four lines of varying thickness the width of cover]</td></tr>
<tr><td>BINDING</td><td>White stiff cartridge paper wraps sewn with white linen thread.</td></tr>
<tr><td>PAPER</td><td>Smooth white Blenheim wove 40 lb crown folio.</td></tr>
<tr><td>NOTES</td><td>Winner of the Newdigate Prize for 1968. Published on 18 November 1968, in an edition of 200 copies. The promotional card for this volume stated the edition consisted of '230 copies in paper covers', but the press ledger indicates an edition of 200 copies and, furthermore, accounts for the sale of all 200 copies. Pages were guillotined by hand, so there may be some discrepancy in measurements between copies.</td></tr>
</table>

One copy examined measured 5 mm longer than the one described above. John Fuller also states that George MacBeth received a copy with incorrect pagination, and such a copy was located by the bibliographer. Sheets number 6 and 7 are misprinted so, when folded, the order of poems is altered. Poems numbered 6 and 7 fall between poems numbered 14 and 15.

SPECIALLY BOUND EDITION

COLLATION Nine sheets measuring 9¼ × 7³⁄₁₆ in. [240 × 183 mm] folded at centre to 7³⁄₁₆ × 4⅝ in. [183 × 120 mm].

JACKET Printed exactly as covers above, but on dark orange yellow (72) Glastonbury Antique wove paper; folded over binding to form jacket.

BINDING 7⁵⁄₁₆ × 4⅞ in. [187 × 124 mm]. Dark yellowish green (137) cloth over boards.

PAPER Bound copies printed on cartridge paper (Daler A series).

NOTES Twelve copies, including paper covers, were specially bound by Prue Fuller. The contents are as A1 above, excepting the imprint page, which includes a numbered limitation and signature by James Fenton. The bound edition was available for sale on 15 February 1969.

A2 **Norman Bryson, *The Swimmer & Other Poems*** (July 1969)

FRONT COVER Norman Bryson | [in very dark green (147)] The | Swimmer | & | Other | Poems | [in black] Sycamore Press

TITLE PAGE Norman Bryson | THE SWIMMER | & OTHER POEMS | Sycamore Press

IMPRINT PAGE Four hundred copies published in 1969 by the Sycamore | Press, 4 Benson Place, Oxford. | Norman Bryson was born in London in 1949, and was | educated at the King's School, Canterbury, and at King's | College, Cambridge, where he is reading English.

COLLATION Three sheets measuring 10⅞ × 8⅛ in. [276 × 206 mm] folded at centre to 8⅛ × 5⁷⁄₁₆ in. [206 × 138 mm]. Unnumbered. [1]: title page. [2]: '*To Hugh Roberts*'. [3–10]: text. [11]: imprint page. [12]: blank.

BACK COVER Blank.

BINDING Two layers of dark orange yellow (72) Glastonbury Antique wove paper wraps bound with two staples. The outer wrap folds over the inner at front and back. Title in dark green (146) with author and publisher in black.

PAPER Glastonbury Antique wove; watermarked.

CONTENTS Poems: 'The Swimmer', 'The Possibility of Touching', 'Two Cabaret Songs', 'Palau', 'St Johns Wood'.

NOTES Published on 18 July 1969. Imprint page lists the edition as 400 copies, but the Sycamore Press ledger book lists the edition at 430 copies. Some copies feature an advertising wrapper [50 × 331 mm] with the price in moderate blue (182) '50 PENCE' and (in black) a quotation from the *Cambridge Review* and an endorsement by James Fenton on the front. The press ledger indicates the wrapper was produced in June 1977.

SPECIALLY BOUND EDITION

COLLATION Three sheets measuring 11¾ × 9¹¹⁄₁₆ in. [300 × 246 mm] folded at centre to 9¹¹⁄₁₆ × 5⅞ in. [246 × 150 mm]. Unnumbered. [1]: title page. [2]: '*To Hugh Roberts*'. [3–10]: text. [11]: imprint page. [12]: blank.

JACKET Printed as covers above and folded over binding.

BINDING Dark brown (59) cloth covers on board measuring 9¹⁵⁄₁₆ × 6⅛ in. (253 × 156 mm).

NOTES As few as two copies were specially bound by Prue Fuller. The contents are as A2 above.

A3	**Anthony Furnivall, *Si tu veux, nous nous aimerons: for Soprano and Piano*** (February 1970)
FRONT COVER	[in strong reddish brown (40)] [line, 181 mm] | ANTHONY FURNIVALL | [line, 181 mm] | Si tu veux, nous nous aimerons | for soprano and piano | [line, 181 mm] | Sycamore Press | [line, 181 mm]
TITLE PAGE	None.
IMPRINT PAGE	None.
COLLATION	One sheet 14⅜ × 9¾ in. [366 × 249 mm] folded at centre to 9¾ × 7³⁄₁₆ in. [249 × 183 mm]. Unnumbered. [1]: blank. [2–3]: text/score. [4]: blank.
BACK COVER	*Sycamore Press, 4 Benson Place, Oxford. Winter 1970*
BINDING	Dark orange yellow (72) Glastonbury Antique wove paper wraps bound with white linen thread. Lettering and lined rules in strong reddish brown (40).
PAPER	Glastonbury Antique white wove; watermarked.
NOTES	Published on 24 February 1970, in an edition of 150 copies. Music sheet attributed to Stéphane Mallarmé and Anthony Furnivall. Dated 'Oxford 25th April 1969'.

A4	**Peter Redgrove, *The Mother the Daughter and the Sighing Bridge*** (December 1970)
FRONT COVER	[four-lines in vivid blue (176) creating a rectangular border (185 × 118 mm)] [in black within rectangular border] PETER REDGROVE | The | Mother | the Daughter | and | the Sighing | Bridge | Sycamore Press
TITLE PAGE	[decorative line, 67 mm] | Peter Redgrove | [decorative line, 67 mm] | [decorative line, 67 mm] | The Mother | the Daughter | and the | Sighing Bridge | [decorative line, 67 mm] |

[decorative line, 67 mm] | Sycamore Press |
[decorative line, 67 mm]

IMPRINT PAGE   *First published 1970 by Sycamore Press | 4 Benson Place Oxford*

COLLATION   Two sheets measuring 11⅝ × 9⁵⁄₁₆ in. [295 × 237 mm] folded at centre to 9⁵⁄₁₆ × 5¹³⁄₁₆ in. [237 × 147 mm]. Unnumbered. [1]: title page. [2]: imprint page. [3–8]: text.

BACK COVER   Blank.

BINDING   Light blue (181) Queen Anne board stiff wraps sewn with dark blue (183) linen thread. Lettered in black with border in vivid blue (176).

PAPER   Smooth white Mellotex double foolscap quarto.

NOTES   Published on 7 December 1970, in an edition of 500 copies. One specimen examined was sewn with white string and consisted of two sheets measuring 11⅝ × 8⅞ in. [295 × 225 mm] folded at centre to 8⅞ × 5¹³⁄₁₆ in. [225 × 147 mm].

SPECIALLY BOUND EDITION (JUNE 1977)

TITLE PAGE   as in A4 above.

IMPRINT PAGE   *Eight copies of the ordinary edition were | printed on hand-made paper and issued in | 1977 in coloured wrappers. This is no. | First published 1970 by Sycamore Press | 4 Benson Place Oxford*

COLLATION   Two sheets measuring 13 × 10 in. [330 × 254 mm] folded at centre to 10 × 6½ in. [254 × 165 mm]. Unnumbered. [1]: title page. [2]: imprint page. [3–8]: text.

BINDING   Covered in marbled paper.

PAPER   Yellowish grey (93) handmade Hayle Mill paper.

NOTES   For this edition, eight copies were printed on handmade Hayle Mill paper at the time of the first edition, except for the limitation statement, which was printed to the imprint page in May or June 1977. Handmade marbled paper was purchased for the cover in May 1977.

A5 **Alastair Fowler,** *Seventeen*
(June 1971)

FRONT COVER [in light grey (264)] SEVEN | [in very deep red (14)]
Alastair Fowler | [in light grey (264)] TEEN | [in
very deep red (14); printed vertically along the
'N' in 'TEEN'] Sycamore Press

TITLE PAGE [deep red (13)] Alastair Fowler | SEVENTEEN |
Sycamore Press

IMPRINT PAGE *First published 1971 by Sycamore Press | 4 Benson*
Place Oxford

COLLATION Five sheets measuring 4¹³⁄₁₆ × 9¼ in. [237 × 124 mm]
folded at centre to 4¹³⁄₁₆ × 4⅝ in. [124 × 119 mm].
Unnumbered. [1]: title page. [2]: imprint page.
[3–19]: text. [20]: blank.

BACK COVER Blank.

BINDING Very light blue (180) stiff paper wraps sewn with
white linen thread. Title in light grey (264) with
author and publisher in very deep red (14).

PAPER Smooth white Mellotex double foolscap quarto.

NOTES Published in June 1971, in an edition of 200 copies.

A6 **Roy Fuller,** *Song Cycle from a Record Sleeve*
(February 1972)

FRONT COVER ROY FULLER | [large vivid reddish orange (34)
image of masks] | [black] Song Cycle from a
Record Sleeve | [vivid reddish orange (34)]
Sycamore Press

TITLE PAGE [deep purplish blue (197)] SONG CYCLE FROM |
A RECORD SLEEVE

IMPRINT PAGE [deep purplish blue (197)] Sixty copies first
published on 11 February 1972, printed and
| sewn by hand on handmade paper at the
Sycamore Press, | 4 Benson Place, Oxford,
numbered and signed by the author. | This is
number [number and signature follow]

COLLATION	Four sheets measuring 9 × 11¼ in. [285 × 230 mm] folded at centre to 9 × 5⅝ in. [230 × 143 mm]. Unnumbered. [1]: title page. [2]: blank. [3–14]: text. [15]: blank. [16]: imprint page.
BACK COVER	Blank.
BINDING	Glastonbury Antique wove white paper wraps sewn with vivid reddish orange linen thread.
PAPER	Grey Hayle Mill 'Charles I' medium (25 lb), watermarked. Top edge left ragged/uncut, and some pages may be cut slightly smaller than others.
NOTES	Published on 11 February 1972, and limited to 60 copies signed by the author. Sycamore Press ledger indicated circa 30 extra copies were produced beyond the 60 numbered copies. Each page of text also contains a circular image: [3]: deep purplish blue (197); [4]: strong greenish yellow (99); [5]: dark red (13); [6]: vivid blue (176); [7]: deep red (13); [8]: moderate olive green (125); [9]: moderate olive green (125); [10]: deep red (13); [11]: vivid blue (176); [12]: dark red (16); [13]: strong greenish yellow (99); [14]: deep purplish blue (197).

A7   David Harsent, *Truce*
(October 1973)

FRONT COVER	[in dark yellowish green (137); rectangle made up of four lines of varying thickness (85 × 50 mm.)] [within rectangle, in dark reddish brown (44)] DAVID HARSENT	[in dark yellowish green (137)] TRUCE	[in dark reddish brown (44)] Sycamore Press
TITLE PAGE	TRUCE
IMPRINT PAGE	Two hundred copies printed by hand in October 1973	at the Sycamore Press, 4 Benson Place, Oxford	numbered and signed by the author [number and signature follow]

COLLATION	Four sheets measuring 12⅞ × 7⁷⁄₁₆ in. [326 × 190 mm] folded at centre to 7⁷⁄₁₆ × 6⁷⁄₁₆ in. [190 × 163 mm]. Unnumbered. [1]: title page. [2]: blank. [3–14]: text. [15]: blank. [16]: imprint page.
BACK COVER	Blank.
BINDING	Two layers of dark orange-yellow Glastonbury Antique wove paper wraps, bound with dark green linen thread. The outer wrap folds over the inner at front and back. Title in dark yellowish green (137) with author and publisher in dark reddish brown (44).
PAPER	Mellotex cream double foolscap quarto.
NOTES	Published on 13 October 1973, in an edition of 200 signed and numbered copies. Signed by Harsent on 13 October 1973. An additional 7 copies were printed to serve as review copies.

A8 **Brigitte Hanf & John Fuller, *A Bestiary: Twenty-Six Linocuts*** (December 1974)

TITLE CARD	A BESTIARY	Twenty-six linocuts by Brigitte Hanf with poems by John Fuller	[signatures of Hanf and Fuller]	[numbered limitation]	A numbered and signed edition of two hundred and fifty copies published in December 1974	Sycamore Press
COLLATION	Individual cards vary slightly in size, but measure approximately 6¼ × 5 in. [160 × 128 mm]. Unnumbered. [title card followed by 26 cards alphabetized by featured animal].
BACK	[each card, excepting title card] Linocut by Brigitte Hanf and poem by John Fuller from a Bestiary published in 1974 by Sycamore Press	4 Benson Place, Oxford
BINDING	None (cards housed in a plastic envelope with a numbered sticker that corresponds to the numbered edition; envelope measures 9¼ × 6⁵⁄₁₆ [235 × 160 mm]).

PAPER	White Ivorex cards.
CONTENTS	A series of 26 cards [27 including title card], each with a drawing and corresponding quatrain of an animal. Animals in alphabetical order are: Ant, Butterfly, Cuckoo, Donkey, Elephant, Fly, Gull, Hedgehog, Inkfish, Jackal, Kangaroo, Lion, Mosquito, Nightingale, Owl, Pelican, Quail, Rat, Swan, Tiger, Unicorn, Viper, Whale, X [a nameless animal], Yak, Zebra.
NOTES	Printed by Oxonian Press. Published on 10 December 1974, in a numbered and signed edition of 250 copies, plus an additional 50 unsigned copies. Illustrations by Hanf with poems by Fuller.

A9 *The Sycamore Miscellany*
(January 1977)

FRONT	[within four ornamental corners] The	[in very deep red (14)] Sycamore	[in black] MISCELLANY	[rule, 75 mm]	[in very deep red (14)] by several hands	[in black; rule, 75 mm]	[in very deep red (14)] *Even the Sycamore with her thousand keys	Could not force locks as intricate as these,	Nor Argus ravel out such mysteries.*	(Walter de la Mare)	[in black; rule, 75 mm]	Sycamore Press	[in very deep red (14)] Oxford	[in black] 1977
COLLATION	Two sheets measuring 8⅜ × 6 in. [214 × 152 mm] folded at centre to 6 × 4³⁄₁₆ in. [107 × 163 mm]. [1]: title page. [2]: *'Fifty copies of this miscellany have been	printed on reconstituted waste paper at	the Sycamore Press, 4 Benson Place, Ox-	ford, to be issued in parts. Not for sale.	This is number'*. [3–8]: text.
BINDING	None.
PAPER	Handmade by John Fuller.
CONTENTS	Miscellaneous verse, including several ribald quatrains about a homosexual King of China.

Unsigned contributions by Jonathan Keates
(p. 3), Roy Fuller (pp. 4–5) and, for the 'King
of China' verses, in the order of appearance,
Nicholas Garland, John Fuller, James Fenton,
Francis Hope, Christopher Hitchens and John
Fuller.

NOTES   Text on pages [2]–8 is printed within a vivid red
(11) rectangle [110 × 77 mm]. Ornamental wood
block printed to the top of page 3, and a line
block image of a king printed in dark green (146)
on page 6. Hand sewn with vivid red (11) linen
thread. Another sheet was printed for pages 9
and 16 with additional 'King of China' verses and
a poem titled 'In Austria'. Though the volume
was never completed there is some indication that
copies of the unfinished page still circulated.

A10   **John Fuller, *Bel and the Dragon***
(June 1977)

FRONT COVER   John Fuller | BEL & the | DRAGON | [drawing in
white] | Sycamore Press

TITLE PAGE   John Fuller | BEL AND THE DRAGON | The
1977 Oxford Prize Poem on a Sacred Subject |
Sycamore Press

IMPRINT PAGE   One hundred and sixty copies printed by hand in
1977 | at the Sycamore Press, 4 Benson Place,
Oxford | numbered and signed by the author
[number and signature follow]

COLLATION   Three sheets measuring 11⅜ × 7⅞ in. [290 × 200
mm] folded at centre to 7⅞ × 5¹¹⁄₁₆ in. [200 × 138
mm]. Unnumbered. [1]: title page. [2]: blank.
[3–9]: text. [10–11]: blank. [12]: imprint page.

BACK COVER   Blank.

BINDING   Strong red (12) woven wraps sewn with white linen
thread. Lettered in black with white image to
front.

PAPER   Abermill Bond wove double foolscap quarto;
watermarked.

A 11   *A Florilegium for John Florio*
(Autumn 1981)

FRONT COVER   A | Florilegium | for | John Florio | [illustration in white] | Sycamore Press

TITLE PAGE   A | Florilegium | for | John Florio | 1981 [text printed within vivid red (11) decorative border (155 × 105 mm)]

IMPRINT PAGE   *These poems were read at the John Florio Society | of Magdalen College, Oxford, and hand-set, printed and sewn | by its members at the Sycamore Press, Oxford, | in an edition of two hundred and forty copies. | Autumn 1981. | The poems are by Claire Andrews, Fernanda Eberstadt, | John Fuller, Alan Hollinghurst, Ignoto, Mick Imlah, Michèle | le Roux, Andrew McCall, Bernard O'Donoghue and Louise Walker.*

COLLATION   Four sheets measuring 10¹¹⁄₁₆ × 8⅛ in. [271 × 206 mm] folded at centre to 8⅛ × 5⅜ in. [206 × 137 mm]. Unnumbered. [1]: title page. [2]: imprint page. [3]: epigraphs. [4]: blank. [5–16]: text.

BACK COVER   Blank.

BINDING   Medium grey (265) paper wraps (175 gsm) sewn with black linen thread. Lettering in black with white image.

PAPER   Colorplan China White (135 gsm) paper; no watermark.

CONTENTS   Twelve poems: 'Landscape', 'Rain', 'Atmosphere', 'Concerto for Double Bass', 'Afternoon', 'Quasimodo says Goodnight', 'Rites of Paysage', 'Epigram', 'The Crab', 'The Derelict Houses at Great Barrington', 'Penelope's Words', 'Prologue'. Poems are unsigned, but authorship has been identified for the following:

Unattributed: 'Landscape', Atmosphere',
'Afternoon' and 'Epigram'
Hollinghurst: 'Rain' and 'The Derelict Houses at
Great Barrington'
Fuller: 'Concerto for Double Bass' and 'Prologue'
Imlah: 'Quasimodo says Goodnight'
Eberstadt: 'Rites of Paysage'
O'Donoghue: 'The Crab'
Le Roux: 'Penelope's Words'

NOTES   Published in Autumn 1981, in an edition of 240
copies. Two small, ornate impressions in vivid
red (11) are printed at the bottom of the final
page.

A12   **James Fenton,** *Dead Soldiers*
(December 1981)

FRONT COVER   JAMES FENTON | Dead Soldiers | [silhouette image
of four 'chess pawns', the last tipped on its side] |
Sycamore Press

TITLE PAGE   James Fenton | DEAD SOLDIERS | Sycamore Press

IMPRINT PAGE   *Printed by hand at the Sycamore Press, 4 Benson*
Place, Oxford. | Copyright James Fenton 1981.

COLLATION   Two sheets measuring 10⅞ × 8³⁄₁₆ in. [276 × 208
mm] folded at centre to 8³⁄₁₆ × 5⁷⁄₁₆ in. [208 × 138
mm]. Unnumbered. [1]: title page. [2]: imprint
page. [3–6]: text. [7–8]: blank.

BACK COVER   Blank.

BINDING   Deep red (13) paper wraps (175 gsm) sewn with
black linen thread.

PAPER   Colorplan China White (135 gsm) paper; no
watermark.

NOTES   Published on 12 December 1981, in an edition of 400
copies.

A13   **Mick Imlah, *The Zoologist's Bath and Other Adventures***
(June 1982)

FRONT COVER   [in dark olive green (126)] MICK IMLAH | The | Zoologist's | Bath | and other | adventures | [image in strong brown (55)] | Sycamore Press

TITLE PAGE   Mick Imlah | The Zoologist's Bath | and other adventures | Sycamore Press

IMPRINT PAGE   *Printed by hand at the Sycamore Press, 4 Benson Place, Oxford | June 1982*

COLLATION   Four sheets measuring 10⅞ × 8⅛ in. [276 × 206 mm] folded at centre to 8⅛ × 5⁷⁄₁₆ in. [206 × 138 mm]. Unnumbered. [1]: title page. [2]: imprint page. [3–15]: text. [16]: blank.

BACK COVER   [image in strong brown (55)] | [in dark olive green (126)] 'A rabbit's foot, gristly | In someone's cabinet.'

BINDING   Pale yellow (89) paper wraps (175 gsm) sewn with dark olive green (126) linen thread.

PAPER   New England White Laid paper (100 gsm); watermarked.

CONTENTS   Poems: 'The Zoologist's Bath', 'Brawl in Co. Kerry', 'Quasimodo says Goodnight', 'Insomnia', 'Abortion', 'Jealousy'.

NOTES   Published on 7 June 1982, in an edition of 400 copies.

A14   ***Poems for Roy Fuller on His Seventieth Birthday***
(February 1982)

FRONT COVER   Poems for | Roy Fuller | on his seventieth birthday | [image of five squares in deep red (13)] | Sycamore Press

TITLE PAGE   Poems for Roy Fuller | on his seventieth birthday | Sycamore Press

IMPRINT PAGE	*Printed by hand at the Sycamore Press, 4 Benson Place, Oxford.*	*11 February 1982*
COLLATION	Three sheets measuring 10⅞ × 8³⁄₁₆ in. [276 × 209 mm] folded at centre to 8³⁄₁₆ × 5⁷⁄₁₆ in. [209 × 138 mm]. Unnumbered. [1]: title page. [2]: imprint page. [3–11]: text. [12]: blank.
BACK COVER	JACK CLARK	AEDAMAIR CLEARY	JOHN FULLER	JOHN LEHMANN	ANTHONY POWELL	ALAN ROSS	STEPHEN SPENDER	JULIAN SYMONS	ANTHONY THWAITE
BINDING	Light bluish grey (190) paper wraps (175 gsm) sewn with red linen thread.
PAPER	Colorplan China White (135 gsm) paper; no watermark.
CONTENTS	Poems: Julian Symons, 'For Roy at Seventy'; John Lehmann, [untitled]; Stephen Spender, 'Lines for Roy Fuller'; Alan Ross, 'Remembering Charlton'; Anthony Powell, 'Building Society Drinking Song'; Aedamair Cleary, 'Letters'; Anthony Thwaite, 'For Roy Fuller at Seventy'; Jack Clark, 'For an Old Codger upon His Seventieth Birthday: From a Codger Nearly as Old'; John Fuller, 'Last Page'.
NOTES	Published on 11 February 1982, in an edition of 300 copies.

A15 **Alan Hollinghurst,** *Confidential Chats with Boys*
(July 1982)

FRONT COVER	ALAN HOLLINGHURST	Confidential	Chats	with Boys	[image]	Sycamore Press
TITLE PAGE	Alan Hollinghurst	CONFIDENTIAL	CHATS	WITH BOYS	Sycamore Press
IMPRINT PAGE	*Printed by hand at the Sycamore Press, 4 Benson Place, Oxford*	*July 1982*
COLLATION	Two sheets measuring 10⅞ × 8³⁄₁₆ in. [276 × 208 mm] folded at centre to 8³⁄₁₆ × 5⁷⁄₁₆ in. [208 × 138

mm]. Unnumbered. [1]: title page. [2]: imprint page. [3–7]: text. [8]: blank.

BACK COVER [smaller version of front cover image]

BINDING Dark purplish red (259) paper wraps (175 gsm) sewn with black linen thread.

PAPER Colorplan China White (135 gsm) paper; no watermark.

NOTES Published on 15 July 1982, in an edition of 300 copies.

A16 Gavin Ewart, *Capital Letters* (July 1983)

FRONT COVER [in dark reddish brown (44)] GAVIN EWART | Capital | Letters | [drawing] | Sycamore Press

TITLE PAGE Gavin Ewart | CAPITAL LETTERS | Sycamore Press | 1983

IMPRINT PAGE *Printed by the Sycamore Press, 4 Benson Place, Oxford. | July 1983*

COLLATION Two sheets measuring 10⅞ × 8⅛ in. [276 × 206 mm] folded at centre to 8⅛ × 5⁷⁄₁₆ in. [206 × 138 mm]. Unnumbered. [1]: title page. [2]: imprint page. [3–7]: text. [8]: blank.

BACK COVER Blank.

BINDING Greyish blue (186) paper wraps (175 gsm) sewn with red linen thread.

PAPER Colorplan China White (135 gsm) paper; no watermark.

NOTES Published on 1 July 1983, in an edition of 400 copies. Text set in Linotype by the Oxonian Press, but printed by hand on the Sycamore Press.

A17	*Noctes Floriosae* (June 1983)
FRONT COVER	Noctes	Floriosae	[illustration in dark olive green (126)]	[in black] Sycamore Press
TITLE PAGE	Noctes Floriosae	Sycamore Press	1983
IMPRINT PAGE	*These poems were read at the John Florio Society	of Magdalen College, Oxford, and hand-set, printed and sewn	by its members at the Sycamore Press, Oxford,	in an edition of two hundred and sixty copies.	Summer 1983.	An earlier collection, A Florilegium for John Florio, was	published in Autumn 1981.	The poems are by Claire Andrews, Oliver Davis, Joanne Dean,	John Fuller, Mick Imlah, Nick Jenkins, Bernard O'Donoghue,	Elise Paschen, Mary Peckham, Jonathan Schutz and Louise Walker.*
COLLATION	Four sheets measuring 10¹⁵⁄₁₆ × 8⅜ in. [277 × 208 mm] folded at centre to 8⅜ × 5½ in. [208 × 139 mm]. Unnumbered. [1]: title page. [2]: imprint page. [3]: epigraphs. [4]: blank. [5–16]: text.
BACK COVER	Blank.
BINDING	Greyish olive green (127) paper wraps (175 gsm) sewn with dark olive green linen thread.
PAPER	Colorplan China White (135 gsm) paper; no watermark.
CONTENTS	Eleven poems: 'Distraction', 'The Front Room', 'Surprise', 'Rendezvous', 'Parallel Lines', 'A Last Dispatch from the Island', 'The Music Between the Notes', 'Secrets', 'The Scene: A Parisian Inn', 'Gold Dragons', 'Visiting St. Anthony'. Poems are unsigned, but authorship has been identified for the following: Unattributed: 'Surprise', 'Parallel Lines', 'A Last Dispatch from the Island', 'The Music Between the Notes', 'Gold Dragons' Fuller: 'Distraction' Paschen: 'The Front Room' Walker: 'Rendezvous'

O'Donoghue: 'Secrets'
Jenkins: 'The Scene: A Parisian Inn'
Imlah: 'Visiting St. Anthony'

<table>
<tr><td>NOTES</td><td>Published in June 1983, in a stated edition of 260 copies. The press ledger states 270 copies were printed.</td></tr>
</table>

A18   **Bernard O'Donoghue, *Razorblades and Pencils*** (February 1984)

FRONT COVER   BERNARD O'DONOGHUE | Razorblades | and | Pencils | [image of five joined squares in moderate olive green (125)] | [in black] Sycamore Press

TITLE PAGE   Bernard O'Donoghue | RAZORBLADES | AND | PENCILS | Sycamore Press

IMPRINT PAGE   *Printed by hand at the Sycamore Press, 4 Benson Place, Oxford | January 1984*

COLLATION   Five sheets measuring 10⅞ × 8⅛ in. [276 × 206 mm] folded at centre to 8⅛ × 5⁷⁄₁₆ in. [206 × 138 mm]. Unnumbered. [1]: title page. [2]: imprint page. [3–19]: text. [20]: blank.

BACK COVER   Blank.

BINDING   Light olive (106) paper wraps (175 gsm) sewn with light olive (106) linen thread. Lettering in black with stamp in moderate olive green (125).

PAPER   Colorplan China White (135 gsm) paper; no watermark.

CONTENTS   Poems: 'Heather', 'Father Christmas', 'Holy Island', 'Aurofac 20', 'Secrets', 'St Patrick's Purgatory', 'The Nuthatch', 'O'Regan the Amateur Anatomist', 'Morning in Beara', 'Beware the Crab', 'St Brigid Night', 'History Remainders', 'Timing the Pigs', 'Nel Mezzo del Cammin', 'A Goliard of the Eighties', 'Vanellus, Vanellus', 'Translated from the East European'.

NOTES   Published on 23 February 1984, in an edition of 400 copies.

A19   Gavin Ewart, *Told of the Existence of an Antique Shop Run by Gavina Ewart* (1984)

FRONT COVER   [pasted to cover, photo of store sign stating, 'GAVINA EWART | ANTIQUES | & | FINE ART']

TITLE PAGE   None.

IMPRINT PAGE   *Sycamore Press, 4 Benson Place, Oxford. 1984.*

COLLATION   One sheet measuring 9 × 6¹¹⁄₁₆ in. [230 × 170 mm] folded at centre to 6¹¹⁄₁₆ × 4½ in. [170 × 115 mm]. Unnumbered. [inside cover]: title page. [opposite title page]: text.

BACK COVER   Blank.

BINDING   Greyish blue (186) paper wraps (175 gsm).

NOTES   Published in 1984, in an edition of 50 copies [based on the fact that 50 photographs are logged in the Sycamore Press ledger]. Specific publication date not listed in the press ledger.

A20   Elise Paschen, *Houses: Coasts* (February 1985)

FRONT COVER   ELISE PASCHEN | Houses: | Coasts | [image in dark blue (183)] | [in black] Sycamore Press

TITLE PAGE   Elise Paschen | HOUSES: | COASTS | Sycamore Press

IMPRINT PAGE   *Printed by hand at the Sycamore Press, 4 Benson Place, Oxford. | February 1985.*

COLLATION   Four sheets measuring 10⅞ × 8⅛ in. [276 × 206 mm] folded at centre to 8⅛ × 5⁷⁄₁₆ in. [206 × 138 mm]. Unnumbered. [1]: title page. [2]: imprint page. [3–15]: text. [16]: blank.

BACK COVER   Blank.

BINDING   Light greenish blue (172) paper wraps (175 gsm) sewn with black linen thread.

PAPER   Colorplan China White (135 gsm) paper; no watermark.

CONTENTS	Poems: 'Oklahoma Home', 'Sea-Gathering', 'Salt Marsh', 'The Front Room', 'Down the Bluff', 'After Afternoon's Nap', 'Details', 'Falling through Snow', 'Moving House', 'On a Plane Flying Down the Coast of Florida', 'Gift', 'Dream', 'Bluebells'.
NOTES	Published on 12 February 1985, in an edition of 400 copies.

A21   Mark Members, *Iron Aspidistra* (December 1985)

FRONT COVER	MARK MEMBERS	Iron	Aspidistra	[image of floret in vivid red (11)]	Sycamore Press
TITLE PAGE	Mark Members	IRON ASPIDISTRA	Sycamore Press
IMPRINT PAGE	*Printed by hand at the Sycamore Press, 4 Benson Place, Oxford.*	21 *December* 1985.
COLLATION	Two sheets measuring 10⅞ × 8³⁄₁₆ in. [276 × 208 mm] folded at centre to 8³⁄₁₆ × 5⁷⁄₁₆ in. [208 × 138 mm]. Unnumbered. [1]: title page. [2]: imprint page. [3]: [publisher's note]. [4–5]: text. [6]: [manuscript reproduction]. [7]: [note on the author]. [8]: blank.
BACK COVER	Blank.
BINDING	Vivid yellow (82) (175 gsm) paper wraps sewn with black linen thread. Lettering in black with an eight-petal image in vivid red (11).
PAPER	Colorplan China White (135 gsm) paper; no watermark.
CONTENTS	Poem with a reproduction of part of the author's manuscript draft of the poem.
NOTES	Published on 21 December 1985, in an edition of 400 copies, 80 of which were presented to Anthony Powell in honour of his eightieth birthday. Roy Fuller adopted the Mark Members pseudonym for this publication.

A22	**Mark Wormald,** *Stills and Reflections* (December 1988)
FRONT COVER	MARK WORMALD	**Stills and**	**Reflections**	 [drawing by Rebecca Dence in white]	Sycamore Press
TITLE PAGE	Mark Wormald	Stills and Reflections	Sycamore Press
IMPRINT PAGE	Stills and Reflections *was the Newdigate Prize Poem* *for 1988.*	*First published at Christmas 1988*	*by* *the Sycamore Press, 4 Benson Place, Oxford*	*Text* *machine-set. Cover printed and sewn by hand at* *the press.*
COLLATION	Three sheets measuring 10¾ × 8⅛ in. [272 × 206 mm] folded at centre to 8⅛ × 5⅜ in. [206 × 136 mm]. Unnumbered. [1]: title page. [2]: imprint page. [3–11]: text. [12]: blank.
BACK COVER	*Cover drawing by Rebecca Dence.*
BINDING	[two versions were printed] Greyish olive green (127) paper wraps (175 gsm) sewn with black string (200 copies). Dark purplish red (259) paper wraps (175 gsm) sewn with black linen thread.
PAPER	Colorplan China White (135 gsm); no watermark.
CONTENTS	Nine pages of text; poems labelled I–VII.
NOTES	The Newdigate Prize poem of 1988, published on 11 December 1988 in an edition of 450 copies. Text was machine-set.

A23	**Gerard Woodward,** *The Unwriter & Other* *Poems* (December 1989)
FRONT COVER	GERARD WOODWARD	The Unwriter	&	other poems	[drawing by Christiania Whitehead in very dark red (17)]	Sycamore Press
TITLE PAGE	Gerard Woodward	The Unwriter	& other poems 	Sycamore Press

IMPRINT PAGE *Acknowledgements are due to* Vision On *('Gloves'),* PN | Review *('Mevagissey Bakery') and* Orbis *('The Kettle's Story').* | *'Suffolk Interior' won fourth prize in the 1987 National* | *Poetry Competition and was broadcast on BBC Radio 3 and* | *Radio Manchester.* | *First published December 1989* | *by the Sycamore Press, 4 Benson Place, Oxford.* | *Text machine-set by Daily Information, Oxford.* | *Cover printed and sewn by hand at the press.*

COLLATION   Four sheets measuring 11 × 8⅛ in. [281 × 206 mm] folded at centre to 8⅛ × 5½ in. [206 × 140 mm]. Unnumbered. [1]: title page. [2]: imprint page. [3–15]: text. [16]: blank.

BACK COVER   *Cover drawing by Christiania Whitehead*

BINDING   Vivid orange (48) paper wraps (175 gsm) sewn with very dark red (17) linen thread. Lettering in black with teapot image in very dark red (17).

PAPER   Colorplan China White (135 gsm); no watermark.

CONTENTS   Poems: 'Suffolk Interior', 'The Dark Mornings', 'Householder', 'Gloves', 'Church Music', 'Family Butchers', 'The Unwriter', 'Window Breaker', 'The Breakfast Table', 'Mevagissey Bakery', 'The Kettle's Story', 'Sink Song'.

NOTES   Printed on 15 December 1989, in an edition of 400 copies. Text was machine-set by Daily Information, Oxford, and the text pages were printed by Presto Print. Examined one specimen that measured 11 × 8³⁄₁₆ in. [281 × 208 mm] folded at centre to 8³⁄₁₆ × 5½ in. [208 × 140 mm].

A24   *A Floribundum*
(February 1991)

FRONT COVER   A | Floribundum | [illustration in white] | Sycamore Press

TITLE PAGE   [within a decorative rectangular border (165 × 123 mm)] A | Floribundum | [drawing by Christiania

Whitehead in blackish red (21)] | Sycamore Press
1990

IMPRINT PAGE *These poems were read at the John Florio Society | of Magdalen College, Oxford, and hand-set, printed, and sewn | by its members at the Sycamore Press, Oxford, | in an edition of two hundred and fifty copies, somewhat | belatedly, after the snows of February 1991. | The poems are by John Fuller, Jane Griffiths, ignoto, John | Leonard, Tim Morton, Fearghus O Conchuir, Bernard | O'Donoghue, Philippa Thomas, Christiania | Whitehead and Mark Wormald. | Drawing by Christiania Whitehead.*

COLLATION Four sheets measuring 11 × 8⅛ in. [280 × 206 mm] folded at centre to 8⅛ × 5½ in. [206 × 140 mm]. Unnumbered. [1]: title page. [2]: imprint page. [3]: epigraphs. [4]: blank. [5–16]: text.

BACK COVER Blank.

BINDING Strong blue (178) paper wraps (175 gsm) sewn with black linen thread. Lettering in black with image in white.

PAPER Colorplan China White (135 gsm); no watermark.

CONTENTS Ten poems: 'Art Class', 'Rules for Retort', 'Anxiety', 'The Vivisector', 'From Bed to Worse', 'In Vino Veritas', 'The Regeneration Game', 'Hope and Hearts', 'Rebecca', 'Ghosts'. Poems are unsigned, but authorship has been identified for the following:

Unattributed: 'Rules for Retort', 'The Vivisector', 'From Bed to Worse', 'The Regeneration Game', 'Ghosts'
Whitehead: 'Art Class'
O'Donoghue: 'In Vino Veritas'
Fuller: 'Hope and Hearts'
Thomas: 'Rebecca'
Wormald: 'Anxiety'

NOTES Printed on 28 February 1991, in an edition of 250 copies.

<table>
<tr><td>A25</td><td>David Harsent, Storybook Hero
(October 1992)</td></tr>
<tr><td>FRONT COVER</td><td>DAVID HARSENT | Storybook | Hero | [illustration in light grey (264)] | [in black] Sycamore Press</td></tr>
<tr><td>TITLE PAGE</td><td>David Harsent | Storybook Hero | Sycamore Press</td></tr>
<tr><td>IMPRINT PAGE</td><td>First Published in 1992 | by the Sycamore Press, 4 Benson Place, Oxford OX2 6QH. | Text machine-set. Cover printed and sewn by hand at the press.</td></tr>
<tr><td>COLLATION</td><td>Six sheets measuring 10⅞ × 8⅛ in. [276 × 206 mm] folded at centre to 8⅛ × 5⁷⁄₁₆ in. [206 × 138 mm]. Unnumbered. [1]: title page. [2]: imprint page. [3]: 'To Harrison Birtwistle'. [4]: blank. [5–24]: text.</td></tr>
<tr><td>BACK COVER</td><td>Blank.</td></tr>
<tr><td>BINDING</td><td>Strong red (12) paper wraps (175 gsm) sewn with black linen thread. Lettering in black with an image in light grey (264).</td></tr>
<tr><td>PAPER</td><td>Colorplan China White (135 gsm); no watermark.</td></tr>
<tr><td>NOTES</td><td>Text pages printed by Presto Print, covers printed by hand. Printed on 15 October 1992, in an edition of 300 copies.</td></tr>
</table>

Broadsheets

<table>
<tr><td>B1</td><td>Roy Fuller, Confrontation Off Korea, 1968
(July 1968)</td></tr>
<tr><td>FRONT</td><td>[when folded] [in vivid red (11)] ROY FULLER | Confrontation Off Korea, 1968 | Sycamore Broadsheet 1</td></tr>
<tr><td>BACK</td><td>[when folded] [in vivid red (11)] [rule, 93 mm] | Sycamore Press, 4 Benson Place, Oxford. Summer 1968</td></tr>
<tr><td>COLLATION</td><td>13 × 8 in. [330 × 203 mm] single sheet folding twice inward to 8 × 4⁵⁄₁₆ in. [203 × 110 mm].</td></tr>
<tr><td>BINDING</td><td>None.</td></tr>
</table>

PAPER   Abermill Bond white wove double foolscap quarto.

CONTENTS   [in black] Single poem in nine stanzas:
             'Confrontation Off Korea, 1968', First line:
             'Return our boat that you've'.

NOTES   Issued in June/July 1968 as number 1 in the series of
             Sycamore Press Broadsheets, in an edition of 250
             copies.

B2   **David Lehman, *Breakfast***
      (August 1968)

FRONT   [when folded] [in moderate blue (182)] DAVID
             LEHMAN | Breakfast | Sycamore Broadsheet 2

BACK   [when folded] [in moderate blue (182)] [biographical
             statement] | [rule, 93 mm] | *Sycamore Press, 4
             Benson Place, Oxford. Summer 1968*

COLLATION   13 × 8 in. [330 × 203 mm] single sheet folding twice
             inward to 8 × 4⁵⁄₁₆ in. [203 × 110 mm].

BINDING   None.

PAPER   Abermill Bond white wove double foolscap quarto.

CONTENTS   [in black] Five poems: 'Breakfast', First line: 'I am
             trembling. You are'; 'Ode', First line: 'I asked a
             fat man,'; 'Cara Mia Katherina', First line: 'I love
             you when I look at you'; 'Activity', First line: 'On
             my way home from work today'; 'Margaret', First
             line: 'You don't get mad often, but when you do'.

NOTES   Issued in August 1968 as number 2 in the series of
             Sycamore Press Broadsheets, in an edition of 300
             copies. Biographical statement consists of five
             lines.

B3   **Harold Massingham, *Creation***
      (August 1968)

FRONT   [when folded] [in dark greyish yellowish brown
             (81)] HAROLD MASSINGHAM | Creation |
             Sycamore Broadsheet 3

BACK	[when folded] [in dark greyish yellowish brown (81)] [biographical statement]	[rule, 93 mm]	*Sycamore Press, 4 Benson Place, Oxford. Summer 1968*
COLLATION	13 × 8 in. [330 × 203 mm] single sheet folding twice inward to 8 × 4⁵⁄₁₆ in. [203 × 110 mm].
BINDING	None.
PAPER	Abermill Bond white wove double foolscap quarto.
CONTENTS	[in black] Single poem: 'Creation', First line: 'Eternally ruling earth,'.
NOTES	Issued in August 1968 as number 3 in the series of Sycamore Press Broadsheets, in an edition of 275 copies. Biographical statement consists of seven lines.

B4 Peter Porter, *Words without Music* (November 1968)

FRONT	[when folded] [in strong orange (50)] PETER PORTER	Words without Music	Sycamore Broadsheet 4
BACK	[when folded] [in strong orange (50)] [biographical statement]	[rule, 93 mm]	*Sycamore Press, 4 Benson Place, Oxford. Autumn* 1968
COLLATION	13 × 8 in. [330 × 203 mm] single sheet folding twice inward to 8 × 4⁵⁄₁₆ in. [203 × 110 mm].
BINDING	None.
PAPER	Abermill Bond white wove double foolscap quarto.
CONTENTS	[in black] Two poems: 'Paroles sans Chant', First line: 'Despairing like a girl who has admitted'; 'Rondo Burlesque', First line: 'Petite, vivacious, eyes green as currency,'.
NOTES	Issued in November 1968 as number 4 in the series of Sycamore Press Broadsheets, in an edition of 450 copies. Biographical statement consists of seven lines.

B5 **Glyn Hughes,** *Almost-Love Poems*
(December 1968)

FRONT [when folded] [in deep yellow green (118)] GLYN
HUGHES | Almost-Love Poems | Sycamore
Broadsheet 5

BACK [when folded] [in deep yellow green (118)]
[biographical statement] | [rule, 93 mm] |
*Sycamore Press, 4 Benson Place, Oxford. Autumn
1968*

COLLATION 13 × 8 in. [330 × 203 mm] single sheet folding twice
inward to 8 × 4⁵⁄₁₆ in. [203 × 110 mm].

BINDING None.

PAPER Abermill Bond white wove double foolscap quarto.

CONTENTS [in black] Two poems: 'Almost-Love Poems', First
line: 'In leather and flowers'; 'Absence', First line:
'Deciding that you are awake, or caught'.

NOTES Issued in December 1968 as number 5 in the series
of Sycamore Press Broadsheets, in an edition of
350 copies. Biographical statement consists of
nine lines.

B6 **Thom Gunn,** *The Fair in the Woods*
(February 1969)

FRONT [when folded] [in very deep red (14)] THOM GUNN
| The Fair in the Woods | Sycamore Broadsheet 6

BACK [when folded] [in very deep red (14)] [biographical
statement] | [rule, 93 mm] | *Sycamore Press, 4
Benson Place, Oxford. Winter 1969*

COLLATION 13 × 8 in. [330 × 203 mm] single sheet folding twice
inward to 8 × 4⁵⁄₁₆ in. [203 × 110 mm].

BINDING None.

PAPER Spicers 21 lb white double foolscap quarto.

CONTENTS [in black] Single poem: 'The Fair in the Woods',
First line: 'The woodsmen blow their horns, and
close the day,'.

NOTES   Issued in February 1969 as number 6 in the series of Sycamore Press Broadsheets, in an edition of 500 copies. Biographical statement consists of five lines.

B7   Alan Brownjohn, *Woman Reading Aloud* (April 1969)

FRONT   [when folded] [in vivid red (11)] ALAN BROWNJOHN | Woman Reading Aloud | Sycamore Broadsheet 7

BACK   [when folded] [in vivid red (11)] [biographical statement] | [rule, 93 mm] | *Sycamore Press, 4 Benson Place, Oxford. Spring 1969*

COLLATION   13 × 8 in. [330 × 203 mm] single sheet folding twice inward to 8 × 4⅚₁₆ in. [203 × 110 mm].

BINDING   None.

PAPER   Abermill Bond white wove double foolscap quarto.

CONTENTS   [in black] Single poem: 'Woman Reading Aloud', First line: 'a tree looked at won't'.

NOTES   Issued in April 1969 as number 7 in the series of Sycamore Press Broadsheets, in an edition of 350 copies. Biographical statement consists of five lines.

B8   James Fenton, *Put Thou Thy Tears Into My Bottle* (June 1969)

FRONT   [when folded] [in blackish blue (188)] JAMES FENTON | Put Thou Thy Tears Into My Bottle | Sycamore Broadsheet 8

BACK   [when folded] [in blackish blue (188)] [biographical statement] | [rule, 93 mm] | *Sycamore Press, 4 Benson Place, Oxford. Summer 1969*

COLLATION   13 × 8 in. [330 × 203 mm] single sheet folding twice inward to 8 × 4⅚₁₆ in. [203 × 110 mm].

BINDING   None.

PAPER	Abermill Bond white wove double foolscap quarto.
CONTENTS	[in black] Two poems: 'One', First line: 'With the blossom and the sunlight'; 'Another One', First line: 'Let us re-weave your torn garments'.
NOTES	Issued in June 1969 as number 8 in the series of Sycamore Press Broadsheets, in an edition of 430 copies. Biographical statement consists of five lines.

B9 David Harsent, *Ashridge*
(December 1969)

FRONT	[when folded] DAVID HARSENT	Ashridge	Sycamore Broadsheet 9
BACK	[when folded] [biographical statement]	[rule, 93 mm]	*Sycamore Press, 4 Benson Place, Oxford. Winter 1970*
COLLATION	13 × 8 in. [330 × 203 mm] single sheet folding twice inward to 8 × 4⁵⁄₁₆ in. [203 × 110 mm].
BINDING	None.
PAPER	Abermill Bond white wove double foolscap quarto.
CONTENTS	Two poems: 'Two Postscripts to my Father', First line: 'As you approached the farmhouse, came'; 'Ashridge', First line: 'The light begins to fade; within the wood'.
NOTES	Issued in December 1969 as number 9 in the series of Sycamore Press Broadsheets, in an edition of 500 copies. Biographical statement consists of one sentence in two lines.

B10 Gregory Rose, *Parables*
(January 1970)

FRONT	[when folded] [in vivid orange yellow (66)] GREGORY ROSE	Parables	Sycamore Broadsheet 10
BACK	[when folded] [in vivid orange yellow (66)] [biographical statement]	[rule, 92 mm]	

Sycamore Press, 4 Benson Place, Oxford. Winter 1970

COLLATION   13 × 8 in. [330 × 203 mm] single sheet folding twice inward to 8 × 4⁵⁄₁₆ in. [203 × 110 mm].

BINDING   None.

PAPER   Abermill Bond white wove double foolscap quarto.

CONTENTS   [in black] Five poems: 'dog dreams', First line: 'it sees a rocket'; 'the dart', First line: 'mesmerised by air'; 'the water', First line: 'the man fills his glass'; 'the numb finger', First line: 'a numb finger'; 'the pebble', First line: 'a pebble'.

NOTES   Issued in January 1970 as number 10 in the series of Sycamore Press Broadsheets, in an edition of 350 copies. Biographical statement consists of one sentence in two lines.

B11   **Bernard Bergonzi, *Memorials***
(March 1970)

FRONT   [when folded] BERNARD BERGONZI | Memorials | Sycamore Broadsheet 11

BACK   [when folded] [biographical statement] | [rule, 92 mm] | *Sycamore Press, 4 Benson Place, Oxford. Spring 1970.*

COLLATION   13 × 8 in. [330 × 203 mm] single sheet folding twice inward to 8 × 4⁵⁄₁₆ in. [203 × 110 mm].

BINDING   None.

PAPER   Abermill Bond white wove double foolscap quarto.

CONTENTS   Three poems: 'East, West', First line: 'It was my daughter's birthday.'; '21 July 1969', First line: 'At dawn the first man walked upon the moon.'; 'The Holly Tree', First line: 'Last year our tree was brilliant'.

NOTES   Issued in March 1970 as number 11 in the series of Sycamore Press Broadsheets, in an edition of 600 copies. Biographical statement consists of six lines.

B12 Peter Levi, *Three Poems*
(May 1970)

FRONT [when folded] [in dark blue (183)] PETER LEVI |
Three Poems | Sycamore Broadsheet 12

BACK [when folded] [in dark blue (183)] [biographical
statement] | [rule, 92 mm] | *Sycamore Press, 4
Benson Place, Oxford. Spring 1970.*

COLLATION 13 × 8 in. [330 × 203 mm] single sheet folding twice
inward to 8 × 4⁵⁄₁₆ in. [203 × 110 mm].

BINDING None.

PAPER Abermill Bond white wove double foolscap quarto.

CONTENTS [in black] Single poem: 'Riddle', First line: 'Without
me there is no person.'.

NOTES Issued in May 1970 as number 12 in the series of
Sycamore Press Broadsheets, in an edition of 500
copies. Biographical statement consists of six
lines.

B13 Michael Schmidt, *One Eye Mirror Cold*
(September 1970)

FRONT [when folded] [in vivid red (11)] Michael Schmidt |
One Eye Mirror Cold | Sycamore Broadsheet 13

BACK [when folded] [in vivid red (11)] [biographical
statement] | [rule, 92 mm] | *Sycamore Press, 4
Benson Place, Oxford. Summer 1970.*

COLLATION 12⁷⁄₁₆ × 7¹⁵⁄₁₆ in. [316 × 202 mm] single sheet folding
twice inward to 7¹⁵⁄₁₆ × 4⅛ in. [202 × 105 mm].

BINDING None.

PAPER Smooth white Mellotex double foolscap quarto.

CONTENTS [in black] Three poems: 'Bedlam and the Oak-
Wood', First line: 'All day it has been windy.
I have stayed'; 'The Gardener', First line: 'If
she looked at a place too long'; 'Canyon of the
Damned', First line: 'When this green earth was
closest to'.

B14   **Gavin Ewart,** *Alphabet Soup*
(February 1971)

FRONT   [when folded] [in very dark yellowish green (138)] Gavin Ewart | Alphabet Soup | Sycamore Broadsheet 14

BACK   [when folded] [in very dark yellowish green (138)] [biographical statement] | [rule, 92 mm] | *Sycamore Press, 4 Benson Place, Oxford. Spring 1971*

COLLATION   12½ × 8 in. [317 × 203 mm] single sheet folding twice inward to 8 × 4³⁄₁₆ in. [203 × 106 mm].

BINDING   None.

PAPER   Smooth white Mellotex double foolscap quarto.

CONTENTS   [in black] Single poem: 'Alphabet Soup', First line: 'Dear Peter, on a summer day'.

NOTES   Issued in February 1971 as number 14 in the series of Sycamore Press Broadsheets, in an edition of 400 copies. Prefaced 'T*he* L*etter to* P. Porter, E*sq.*, 10 *June* 1970'. Biographical statement consists of five lines.

B15   **Peter Redgrove,** *The Bedside Clock*
(July 1971)

FRONT   [when folded] [in deep orange yellow (69)] Peter Redgrove | The Bedside Clock | Sycamore Broadsheet 15

BACK   [when folded] [in deep orange yellow (69)] [biographical statement] | [rule, 92 mm] | *Sycamore Press, 4 Benson Place, Oxford. Summer 1971*

COLLATION   12½ × 8 in. [317 × 203 mm] single sheet folding twice inward to 8 × 4³⁄₁₆ in. [203 × 105.5 mm].

BINDING	None.
PAPER	Smooth white Mellotex double foolscap quarto.
CONTENTS	[in black] Single poem: 'The Bedside Clock', First line: 'I hear the sparks'.
NOTES	Issued in July 1971 as number 15 in the series of Sycamore Press Broadsheets, in an edition of 400 copies. Biographical statement consists of five lines.

B16 **Peter Scupham,** *Children Dancing*
(September 1971)

FRONT	[when folded] [in deep red (13)] Peter Scupham | Children Dancing | Sycamore Broadsheet 16
BACK	[when folded] [in deep red (13)] [biographical statement] | [rule, 92 mm] | *Sycamore Press, 4 Benson Place, Oxford. Summer 1971*
COLLATION	12⅜ × 8 in. [315 × 203 mm] single sheet folding twice inward to 8 × 4⅛ in. [203 × 105 mm].
BINDING	None.
PAPER	Smooth white Mellotex double foolscap quarto.
CONTENTS	[in black] Poem in three parts: 1, First line: 'What shall we throw down'; 2, First line: 'The cracks in an old floor'; 3, First line: 'Shadow and exhaustion overtake us'.
NOTES	Issued in September 1971 as number 16 in the series of Sycamore Press Broadsheets, in an edition of 350 copies. Biographical statement consists of four lines.

B17 **John Mole,** *Something about Love*
(March 1972)

FRONT	[when folded] [in moderate olive green (125)] John Mole | Something about Love | Sycamore Broadsheet 17
BACK	[when folded] [in moderate olive green (125)] [biographical statement] | [rule, 92 mm] |

Sycamore Press, 4 Benson Place, Oxford. Spring 1972

COLLATION 12⅜ × 8 in. [315 × 203 mm] single sheet folding twice inward to 8 × 4⅛ in. [203 × 105 mm].

BINDING None.

PAPER Smooth white Mellotex double foolscap quarto.

CONTENTS [in black] Three poems: 'Pumpkins', First line: 'All night on lamplit doorsteps'; 'Four Cities', First lines: *'Washington DC* | Having sailed to ask her'; 'Beer Cans', First line: 'Catching the light'.

NOTES Issued in March 1972 as number 17 in the series of Sycamore Press Broadsheets, in an edition of 350 copies. Biographical statement consists of four lines.

B18 **Nancy K. Sandars,** *Idling On*
(October 1972)

FRONT [when folded] [in dark blue (183)] N. K. Sandars | Idling On | Sycamore Broadsheet 18

BACK [when folded] [in dark blue (183)] [biographical statement] | [rule, 92 mm] | *Sycamore Press, 4 Benson Place, Oxford. Autumn 1972*

COLLATION 12⅜ × 8 in. [315 × 203 mm] single sheet folding twice inward to 8 × 4⅛ in. [203 × 105 mm].

BINDING None.

PAPER Smooth white Mellotex double foolscap quarto.

CONTENTS [in black] Two poems: 'Grandmother's Steps', First line: 'The children's games were lives of men and women'; 'Idling On', First line: 'All day the talk goes idling on,'.

NOTES Issued in October 1972 as number 18 in the series of Sycamore Press Broadsheets, in an edition of 350 copies. Biographical statement consists of six lines.

B19   **John Cotton,** *Photographs*
(April 1973)

FRONT   [when folded] [in dark greyish yellowish brown (81)] John Cotton | Photographs | Sycamore Broadsheet 19

BACK   [when folded] [in dark greyish yellowish brown (81)] [biographical statement] | [rule, 92 mm] | *Sycamore Press, 4 Benson Place, Oxford. Spring 1973*

COLLATION   13 × 8 in. [330 × 203 mm] single sheet folding twice inward to 8 × 4⁵⁄₁₆ in. [203 × 110 mm].

BINDING   None.

PAPER   Smooth white Mellotex double foolscap quarto.

CONTENTS   [in black] Three poems: 'Keith Douglas', First line: 'I lean against my car'; 'Gertrude Stein and Alice Toklas plus one', First line: 'In the picture they are sitting in St. Mark's Square,'; 'First Love', First line: 'A photograph moves one to remember'.

NOTES   Issued in April 1973 as number 19 in the series of Sycamore Press Broadsheets, in an edition of 350 copies. Biographical statement consists of six lines.

B20   **Roger Mitchell,** *Edges*
(May 1973)

FRONT   [when folded] [in moderate olive green (125)] Roger Mitchell | Edges | Sycamore Broadsheet 20

BACK   [when folded] [in moderate olive green (125)] [biographical statement] | [rule, 92 mm] | *Sycamore Press, 4 Benson Place, Oxford. Summer 1973*

COLLATION   13 × 8 in. [330 × 203 mm] single sheet folding twice inward to 8 × 4⁵⁄₁₆ in. [203 × 110 mm].

BINDING   None.

PAPER   Smooth white Mellotex double foolscap quarto.

<dl>
<dt>CONTENTS</dt>
<dd>[in black] Poem in five parts: 1, First line: 'For months I have walked this rocky coast,'; 2, First line: 'I am never far from edges'; 3, First line: 'This is the time before time'; 4, First line: 'I lie on the hot sand for hours,'; 5, First line: 'The whales have drifted away,'.</dd>

<dt>NOTES</dt>
<dd>Issued in May 1973 as number 20 in the series of Sycamore Press Broadsheets, in an edition of 370 copies. Biographical statement consists of three lines.</dd>
</dl>

B21 Douglas Dunn, *Corporal Punishment* (April 1975)

<dl>
<dt>FRONT</dt>
<dd>[when folded] [in vivid red (11)] Douglas Dunn | Corporal Punishment | Sycamore Broadsheet 21</dd>

<dt>BACK</dt>
<dd>[when folded] [in vivid red (11)] [biographical statement] | [rule, 92 mm] | *Sycamore Press, 4 Benson Place, Oxford. Summer 1975*</dd>

<dt>COLLATION</dt>
<dd>13 × 8 in. [330 × 203 mm] single sheet folding twice inward to 8 × 4�5⁄16 in. [203 × 110 mm].</dd>

<dt>BINDING</dt>
<dd>None.</dd>

<dt>PAPER</dt>
<dd>Smooth white Mellotex double foolscap quarto.</dd>

<dt>CONTENTS</dt>
<dd>[in black] Poem in three parts: 1, First line: 'A thought strikes me'; 2, First line: 'A thought strikes me'; 3, First line: 'On the soft underside'.</dd>

<dt>NOTES</dt>
<dd>Issued in April 1975 as number 21 in the series of Sycamore Press Broadsheets, in an edition of 350 copies. Biographical statement consists of three lines.</dd>
</dl>

B22 Alan Hollinghurst, *Isherwood is at Santa Monica* (December 1975)

<dl>
<dt>FRONT</dt>
<dd>[when folded] [in moderate reddish brown (43)] Alan Hollinghurst | Isherwood is at Santa Monica | Sycamore Broadsheet 22</dd>
</dl>

BACK [when folded] [in moderate reddish brown (43)] [biographical statement] | [rule, 92 mm] | *Sycamore Press, 4 Benson Place, Oxford. Autumn 1975*

COLLATION 13 × 8 in. [330 × 203 mm] single sheet folding twice inward to 8 × 4⁵⁄₁₆ in. [203 × 110 mm].

BINDING None.

PAPER Smooth white Mellotex double foolscap quarto.

CONTENTS [in black] Two poems: 'Isherwood is at Santa Monica', First line: 'Isherwood is at Santa Monica'; 'The Well', First line: 'As deep and as old as the village'.

NOTES Issued in December 1975 as number 22 in the series of Sycamore Press Broadsheets, in an edition of 350 copies. Biographical statement consists of four lines.

B23 **W.H. Auden, *Sue***
(January 1977)

FRONT [when folded] [in blackish blue (188)] W. H. Auden | Sue | Sycamore Broadsheet 23

BACK [when folded] [in blackish blue (188)] [biographical statement] | [rule, 92 mm] | *Sycamore Press, 4 Benson Place, Oxford. Spring 1977*

COLLATION 13 × 8 in. [330 × 203 mm] single sheet folding twice inward to 8 × 4⁵⁄₁₆ in. [203 × 110 mm].

BINDING None.

PAPER Smooth white Mellotex double foolscap quarto.

CONTENTS [in black] Single poem: 'Sue', First line: 'Once upon a time there was a girl named Sue.'

NOTES Issued in January 1977 as number 23 in the series of Sycamore Press Broadsheets, in an edition of 580 copies. Biographical statement consists of twelve lines, including the following information regarding the poem: '[Sue] is previously unpublished. It has been transcribed as accurately as possible, with a number of guesses and reconstructed phrases, from an often barely-legible draft in a notebook belonging to Christopher Isherwood.'

B24   **Andrew Motion, *The Pleasure Steamers*** (February 1977)

FRONT   [when folded] [in moderate reddish brown (43)] Andrew Motion | The Pleasure Steamers | Sycamore Broadsheet 24

BACK   [when folded] [in moderate reddish brown (43)] [biographical statement] | [rule, 92 mm] | *Sycamore Press, 4 Benson Place, Oxford. Spring 1977*

COLLATION   13 × 8 in. [330 × 203 mm] single sheet folding twice inward to 8 × 4⁵⁄₁₆ in. [203 × 110 mm].

BINDING   None.

PAPER   Smooth white Mellotex double foolscap quarto.

CONTENTS   [in black] Poem in three parts: 1, First line: 'It's blowing cold from the east'; 2, First line: 'The river repeats itself, and I'; 3, First line: 'The steamers are ready:'.

NOTES   Issued in February 1977 as number 24 in the series of Sycamore Press Broadsheets, in an edition of 400 copies. Biographical statement consists of six lines.

B25   **Michael Vince, *The Embrace*** (July 1977)

FRONT   [when folded] [in vivid red (11)] Michael Vince | The Embrace | Sycamore Broadsheet 25

BACK   [when folded] [in vivid red (11)] [biographical statement] | [rule, 92 mm] | *Sycamore Press, 4 Benson Place, Oxford. Summer 1977*

COLLATION   13 × 8 in. [330 × 203 mm] single sheet folding twice inward to 8 × 4⁵⁄₁₆ in. [203 × 110 mm].

BINDING   None.

PAPER Smooth white Mellotex double foolscap quarto.

CONTENTS [in black] Single poem: 'The Embrace', First line: 'Seeking her can be to lose the way.'

NOTES Issued in July 1977 as number 25 in the series of Sycamore Press Broadsheets, in an edition of 400 copies. Biographical statement consists of two lines.

B26 **Edward Larrissy, *Three Poems*** (November 1977)

FRONT [when folded] [in dark yellowish green (137)] Edward Larrissy | Three Poems | Sycamore Broadsheet 26

BACK [when folded] [in dark yellowish green (137)] [biographical statement] | [rule, 92 mm] | *Sycamore Press, 4 Benson Place, Oxford. Autumn 1977*

COLLATION 13 × 8 in. [330 × 203 mm] single sheet folding twice inward to 8 × 4⁵⁄₁₆ in. [203 × 110 mm].

BINDING None.

PAPER Smooth white Mellotex double foolscap quarto.

CONTENTS [in black] Three poems: 'The Librarian', First line: 'How melodious he is, the spruce young'; 'Theory of Being', First line: 'I'm easily downcast, you know, and wet days'; 'Portrait of a Lady', First line: 'All these things keep coming at me,'.

NOTES Issued in November 1977 as number 26 in the series of Sycamore Press Broadsheets, in an edition of 400 copies. Biographical statement consists of four lines.

B27 **Philip Larkin, *Femmes Damnées*** (June 1978)

FRONT [when folded] [in deep blue (179)] Philip Larkin | Femmes Damnées | Sycamore Broadsheet 27

<dl>
<dt>BACK</dt>
<dd>[when folded] [in deep blue (179)] [biographical statement] | [rule, 92 mm] | Sycamore Press, 4 Benson Place, Oxford. Summer 1978</dd>

<dt>COLLATION</dt>
<dd>13 × 8⅛ in. [330 × 207 mm] single sheet folding twice inward to 8⅛ × 4⁵⁄₁₆ in. [207 × 110 mm].</dd>

<dt>BINDING</dt>
<dd>None.</dd>

<dt>PAPER</dt>
<dd>Smooth white Mellotex double foolscap quarto.</dd>

<dt>CONTENTS</dt>
<dd>[in black] Single poem: 'Femmes Damnées'. First line: 'The fire is ash: the early morning sun'.</dd>

<dt>NOTES</dt>
<dd>Issued in June 1978 as number 27 in the series of Sycamore Press Broadsheets, in an edition of 400 copies. Biographical statement consists of four lines followed by an excerpt from a note by Larkin: 'Of the present poem, written in 1943, he says: "The piece is evidence that I once read at least one 'foreign poem', though I can't remember how far, if at all, my verses are based on the original." '</dd>
</dl>

B28   **Craig Raine,** *A Journey to Greece*
(Winter 1979)

<dl>
<dt>FRONT</dt>
<dd>[when folded] [in moderate olive brown (95)] Craig Raine | A Journey to Greece | Sycamore Broadsheet 28</dd>

<dt>BACK</dt>
<dd>[when folded] [in moderate olive brown (95)] [biographical statement] | [rule, 92 mm] | Sycamore Press, 4 Benson Place, Oxford. Winter 1979</dd>

<dt>COLLATION</dt>
<dd>13 × 8⅛ in. [330 × 207 mm] single sheet folding twice inward to 8⅛ × 4⁵⁄₁₆ in. [207 × 110 mm].</dd>

<dt>BINDING</dt>
<dd>None.</dd>

<dt>PAPER</dt>
<dd>Smooth white Mellotex double foolscap quarto.</dd>

<dt>CONTENTS</dt>
<dd>[in black] Single poem in six parts: 'A Journey to Greece'. Part 1: 'Monocular'; Part 2: 'Mad Dogs and Englishmen'; Part 3: 'Sleepies'; Part 4: 'Between Two Schools'; Part 5: 'Moly'; Part 6: 'Penelope'.</dd>
</dl>

NOTES   Issued in winter 1979 as number 28 in the series of Sycamore Press Broadsheets, in an edition of 275 copies. Biographical statement consists of two lines.

B29   **Richard Freeman,** *Swimming 1949*
(September 1980)

FRONT   [when folded] [in deep reddish brown (41)] Richard Freeman | Swimming 1949 | Sycamore Broadsheet 29

BACK   [when folded] [in deep reddish brown (41)] [biographical statement] | [rule, 92 mm] | *Sycamore Press, 4 Benson Place, Oxford. Autumn 1980*

COLLATION   13 × 8 in. [330 × 203 mm] single sheet folding twice inward to 8 × 4⁵⁄₁₆ in. [203 × 110 mm].

BINDING   None.

PAPER   Smooth white Mellotex double foolscap quarto.

CONTENTS   [in black] Single poem: 'Swimming 1949', First line: 'The landing stage was as empty as a slice of bread.'

NOTES   Issued around September 1980 as number 29 in the series of Sycamore Press Broadsheets, in an edition of 440 copies. Biographical statement consists of six lines.

B30   **Ted Burford,** *Two Poems*
(July 1983)

FRONT   [when folded] [in vivid red (11)] Ted Burford | Two Poems | Sycamore Broadsheet 30

BACK   [when folded] [in vivid red (11)] [biographical statement] | [rule, 92 mm] | *Sycamore Press, 4 Benson Place, Oxford. Summer 1983.*

COLLATION   13 × 8 in. [330 × 203 mm] single sheet folding twice inward to 8 × 4⁵⁄₁₆ in. [203 × 110 mm].

BINDING   None.

PAPER   Smooth white Mellotex double foolscap quarto.

CONTENTS   [in black] Two poems: 'The House', First line: 'Where, before him'; 'Staying over at Southgate Road', First line: 'I said goodnight to her'.

NOTES   Issued in July 1983 as number 30 in the series of Sycamore Press Broadsheets, in an edition of 400 copies. Biographical statement consists of seven lines.

B31   **Set of Broadsheets 1–12**
             (1970)

FRONT   [when folded] [in dark blue (183)] **Sycamore** | **Broadsheets** | [in moderate reddish brown (43)] thirty-five poems by | ROY FULLER | DAVID LEHMAN | HAROLD MASSINGHAM | PETER PORTER | GLYN HUGHES | THOM GUNN | ALAN BROWNJOHN | JAMES FENTON | DAVID HARSENT | GREGORY ROSE | BERNARD BERGONZI | PETER LEVI | [art block in dark blue (183)] | [in moderate reddish brown (43)] Numbers 1 to 12 complete | [in dark blue (183)] **1968 - 1970**

BACK   [when folded] [embossed at top] Croxley Cartridge | A John Dickinson Product

COLLATION   9¾₁₆ × 4¾ in. [233 × 120 mm].

BINDING   None.

PAPER   Smooth white Croxley Cartridge envelope.

CONTENTS   A copy of Sycamore Press Broadsheets 1–12.

NOTES   Sets of Sycamore Press Broadsheets 1–12 were created in 1970. The press purchased 100 envelopes to house the broadsheets, though records also indicate as few as 30 of each broadsheet were held back for sets.

B32   **Set of Broadsheets 13–24**
       (1977)

FRONT   [in moderate reddish brown (43)] **Sycamore
         Broadsheets 13–24** | Poems by: Michael Schmidt,
         Gavin Ewart, | Peter Redgrove, Peter Scupham,
         John Mole, | N. K. Sandars, John Cotton, Roger
         Mitchell, | Douglas Dunn, Alan Hollinghurst,
         | W. H. Auden and Andrew Motion. [A small
         device in black is printed on the right and left
         side of the last two lines of author names.]

BACK   [blank]

COLLATION   9³⁄₁₆ × 4¾ in. [233 × 120 mm].

BINDING   None.

PAPER   Smooth white envelope.

CONTENTS   A copy of Sycamore Press Broadsheets 13–24.

NOTES   Sets of Broadsheets 13–24 were created in February
            1977. The press purchased 70 envelopes to house
            the broadsheets, but created only about 48 sets.

B33   **Set of Broadsheets 1–30**
       (1988–89)

BINDING   Greyish olive (110) clamshell box stamped in gold
            vertically to spine: '[two rules, width of spine]
            SYCAMORE BROADSHEETS 1968–1983 [two
            rules, width of spine]'. Box measures 8¾ × 4¹⁵⁄₁₆
            × 1¹⁄₁₆ [223 × 126 × 27 mm].

CONTENTS   A complete set of Sycamore Press Broadsheets 1–30.

NOTES   Six sets of Broadsheets 1–30 were created and
            housed in specially made boxes. Inside of box
            is stamped 'made by maltby.oxford'. Initially,
            only two sets were offered for sale at £180 each.
            The invoice for the first set sold was dated 16
            February 1989. The second set was invoiced on
            26 November 1989. Sycamore Press Newsletter
            No. 2 (December 1989) states that the two sets
            for sale sold quickly, which, given the date of the

first invoice, suggests the boxes were most likely constructed in late 1988 or early 1989.

Card series

C1 **Andrew McNeillie and Julian Bell,** *Corncrake* **(May 1973)**

FRONT CORNCRAKE | [text in three stanzas] | [drawing]

BACK [printed on left side, perpendicular to bottom of card] *Sycamore Card 1: Poem by Andrew McNeillie. Drawing by Julian Bell.* | *Sycamore Press, 4 Benson Place, Oxford.*

COLLATION Single card measuring 6½ × 4¾ in. [165 × 122 mm].

BINDING None.

PAPER White Ivorex card.

CONTENTS Poem by Andrew McNeillie with a drawing by Julian Bell.

NOTES Issued in May 1973 as number 1 in the series of Sycamore Press Postcards in an edition of 250 copies.

C2 *Morphy v. Duke of Brunswick* (September/October 1974)

FRONT [image of man with bent elbow printed in moderate blue (182) to left] [series of seventeen numbered chess moves with illustrated chess board placed between moves fifteen and sixteen, in black to right]

BACK [in black to right side, perpendicular to bottom of card] *Sycamore Card 2: Paul Morphy plays the Duke of Brunswick and Count Isouard* | *in the Duke's box in the Paris Opera House during a performance of Rossini, 1858.* | *Sycamore Press, 4 Benson Place, Oxford.*

COLLATION Single card measuring 6½ × 4¾ in. [165 × 122 mm].

BINDING	None.
PAPER	White Ivorex card.
CONTENTS	Image as described above.
NOTES	Issued in September/October 1974 as number 2 in the series of Sycamore Press Postcards in an edition of 250 copies.

c3 Alastair Fowler, *Helen's Topless Towers* (April 1975)

FRONT	[in vivid red (11), 32 lines of text shaped as a torso]
BACK	[in black to right side, perpendicular to bottom of card] *Sycamore Card 3: Helen's Topless Towers by Alastair Fowler.	Sycamore Press, 4 Benson Place, Oxford.*
COLLATION	Single card measuring 6⅜ × 4¾ in. [162 × 122 mm].
BINDING	None.
PAPER	White Ivorex card.
NOTES	Issued in April 1975 as number 3 in the series of Sycamore Press Postcards in an edition of 250 copies.

c4 Gavin Ewart, *Indian Love Lyric* (July 1976)

FRONT	[in vivid red (11)] The Indian Love Lyric	[two lines of poem]	[in black] [one line of poem]	[large image in black and vivid red (11)]	[in white] [two lines of poem]
BACK	[in black to right side, perpendicular to bottom of card] *Sycamore Card 4: Poem by Gavin Ewart. Drawing by Brigitte Hanf.	Sycamore Press, 4 Benson Place, Oxford.*
COLLATION	Single card measuring 6½ × 4¾ in. [165 × 122 mm].
BINDING	None.
PAPER	White Ivorex card.

NOTES   Issued in July 1976 as number 4 in the series of Sycamore Press Postcards in an edition of 275 copies.

C5   **Laurence Lerner,** *Definition of Love* (January 1977)

FRONT   [in medium grey (265); 12–line poem]

BACK   [in black to bottom] *Sycamore Card 5: Definition of Love by Laurence Lerner. | Sycamore Press, 4 Benson Place, Oxford.*

COLLATION   Single card measuring 5¼ × 6⅜ in. [133 × 162 mm].

BINDING   None.

PAPER   White Ivorex card.

NOTES   Issued in January 1977 as number 5 in the series of Sycamore Press Postcards in an edition of 250 copies. Fuller used Mecanorma Letterpress sheets for the font.

C6   **Bryan Kelly and John Fuller,** *Canon* (June 1977)

FRONT   Allegro | [circular music notations with lyrics in black] | [four scroll-work corner pieces frame the card in deep reddish orange (36)]

BACK   [in black to right side, perpendicular to bottom of card] *Sycamore Card 6: A Christmas Canon by Bryan Kelly and John Fuller. | Sycamore Press, 4 Benson Place, Oxford.*

COLLATION   Single card measuring 6½ × 5¼ in. [165 × 133 mm].

BINDING   None.

PAPER   White Ivorex card.

CONTENTS   Music notations with lyrics.

NOTES   Issued around June 1977 as number 6 in the series of Sycamore Press Postcards in an edition of 400 copies. Fuller used Mecanorma Letterpress sheets for the sheet music font.

C7	Ian Caws, *Cathy's Clutter* (October 1978)
FRONT	[four stanzas of four lines each, printed in black; poem framed with artwork printed in dark blue (183)]
BACK	[in black to right side, perpendicular to bottom of card] *Sycamore Card 7: Cathy's Clutter by Ian Caws. Drawing by Adam Thorpe.*	*Sycamore Press, 4 Benson Place, Oxford.*
COLLATION	Single card measuring 6½ × 5¼ in. [165 × 133 mm].
BINDING	None.
PAPER	White Ivorex card.
CONTENTS	Poem accompanied with artwork of frog and various animals, a clock, and playing cards.
NOTES	Issued around October 1978 as number 7 in the series of Sycamore Press Postcards in an edition of 400 copies.

Card advertisements
& Nemo's Almanac

Promotional cards were typically printed on standard postcard stock bearing preprinted text to one side. The colour of this preprinted text is not designated in the descriptions that follow.

John Fuller edited *Nemo's Almanac* from 1971 to 1987, but the competition was printed under the auspices of the Sycamore Press only from 1971 to 1978. While later issues often contain advertisements for Sycamore Press publications, only issues from 1971 to 1978, featuring 'Sycamore Press' on their covers, are described below.

D1	Advertisement for *Our Western Furniture* by James Fenton (1968)
FRONT	[in deep yellowish green (132)] Sycamore Press	announce the publication of the Newdigate

Prize | Poem for 1968 | [rule, 75 mm] | OUR WESTERN FURNITURE | by JAMES FENTON | [rule, 75 mm] | This sequence of twenty-one sonnets investigates | with a descriptive delicacy and moving irony one | of the earliest examples of American gunboat dip- | lomacy. James Fenton was born in 1949 and is | reading philosophy and psychology at Magdalen | College, Oxford. | [rule, 75 mm] | 230 copies in paper covers, at 5s post free (32pp.) | Booksellers: six copies for a pound. | [rule, 75 mm] | *To the Sycamore Press, 4 Benson Place, Oxford. | Please send me copies of* Our Western Furniture. | *Signed: | Address: | I enclose a cheque or p.o. for*

BACK   POST CARD | THE ADDRESS TO BE WRITTEN ON THIS SIDE [rectangle to upper right (23 × 19 mm)]

COLLATION   Single card measuring 5½ × 3½ in. [141 × 89 mm].

PAPER   Standard white postcard stock.

NOTES   Printed in October or November 1968. Edition is not specified, but the press ledger indicates 100 cards were purchased for publicity purposes on 11 October 1968, and 20 cards were mailed on 29 November 1968.

D2   **The Poetry Chair** (1968)

FRONT   The Poetry Chair | Votes may be cast in the Sheldonian Theatre on | Thursday 21 November at 9.30 to 10.30 a.m., 1.45 to | 2.45 p.m., and 3.30 to 4.30 p.m., and on Saturday 23 | November at 12.15 to 12.45 p.m. and 3.30 to 4.30 p.m. | An M.A. gown only is needed. | We hope you will give your support to ROY FULLER | who has been nominated by J. J. G. Alexander, King- | sley Amis, W. H. Auden, F. W. Bateson, Dorothy | Bednarowska, Bernard Bergonzi, John Carey, Cecil | Day-Lewis, John Fuller, J. R. Gilling, J. Griffin, Sir | William Hayter, R. W. Hunt, Philip Larkin, Peter | Levi, Anthony Levi, George

MacBeth, Angus Mac- | intyre, Julian Mitchell, Charles Monteith, R. C. Ock- | enden, Anthony Powell, Anthony Quinton, M. E. | Reeves, Christopher Ricks, Anthony Thwaite, John | Wain and Stephen Wall.

BACK   POST CARD | THE ADDRESS TO BE WRITTEN ON THIS SIDE [rectangle to upper right (23 × 19 mm)]

COLLATION   Single card measuring 5½ × 3½ in. [141 × 89 mm].

PAPER   Standard white postcard stock.

NOTES   Printed in late 1968, in an unspecified number of copies. On 21 November 1968, Roy Fuller was elected to serve as the Oxford Poetry Chair. He served from 1968 to 1973.

D3   **Advertisement for Sycamore Press publications (1969)**

FRONT   Sycamore Press 1969 | announce the publication of a striking first collection | THE SWIMMER AND OTHER POEMS | by NORMAN BRYSON *July, 5s* | [rule, 76 mm] | already published is | OUR WESTERN FURNITURE | by JAMES FENTON *5s* | [rule, 76 mm] | and in a broadsheet series (*1 and 2 are out of print*) | 1 Roy Fuller *Confrontation off Korea 1968* | 2 David Lehman *Breakfast* | 3 Harold Massingham *Creation* | 4 Peter Porter *Words without Music* | 5 Glyn Hughes *Almost-Love Poems* | 6 Thom Gunn *The Fair in the Woods* | 7 Alan Brownjohn *Woman Reading Aloud* | *9d each* | [dotted rule, 76 mm] | To the Sycamore Press, 4 Benson Place, Oxford | I enclose   for   copies of | I enclose 10s for 14 broadsheets starting with no: | Name: | Address:

BACK   POST CARD | THE ADDRESS TO BE WRITTEN ON THIS SIDE [rectangle to upper right (23 × 19 mm.)]

COLLATION   Single card measuring 5½ × 3½ in. [141 × 89 mm].

PAPER   Standard white postcard stock.

NOTES   Printed in May or June 1969. Edition is not specified, but the press ledger indicates 400 cards were purchased for publicity purposes on 27 April 1969, and 59 cards were mailed on 30 June 1969.

D4   **Advertisement for *Nemo's Almanac* 1971** (September 1970)

FRONT   [four vertical rules of decreasing thickness from top to bottom of card] NEMO | [image of two men, the left with a cane] | [in vivid red (11)] *"What is* Nemo? *Your ignorance ſur- | priſes me. Why, Sir, when a man is tired of* Nemo, *he is tired of life; for there is* | [in black; four vertical rules of increasing thickness from top to bottom of card] [in vivid red (11); printed perpendicular to image of men] *in* Nemo *all that life can afford." | The Doctor then fell into a profound ſilence, after | which he reſumed; "Yet I have three quotations to | diſcover ſtill. Upon my life I do not know them." | "Indeed (I ſaid) you are too late. The priſes are | announced and the new* Nemo *already on ſale." | He at once ſeized my arm, and we haſtened to the |* Sycamore Preſs *at* 4 Benſon Place, Oxford, *where | for five ſhillings the lateſt* Nemo *was ours.*

BACK   POST CARD | THE ADDRESS TO BE WRITTEN ON THIS SIDE [rectangle to upper right (23 × 19 mm.)]

COLLATION   Single card measuring 5½ × 3½ in. [141 × 89 mm].

PAPER   Standard white postcard stock.

NOTES   Printed in September 1970. Edition is not specified, but the press ledger indicates approximately 100 cards were mailed on 30 September 1970.

D5   *Nemo's Almanac 1971* (October 1970)

FRONT COVER   NEMO'S ALMANAC 1971 | *A literary competition in its 80th year* | [line, 120 mm] | "He wrapped himself in quotations— | as a beggar would enfold himself in | the purple of Emperors." | [line, 120 mm] | Sycamore Press 25p

TITLE PAGE [in double ruled box 92 × 31 mm] NEMO'S ALMANAC 1971 | *Edited by John Fuller* | *Sycamore Press, 4 Benson Place, Oxford* | [competition rules] | [statement regarding marks and prizes]

IMPRINT PAGE None.

COLLATION Eight sheets 9⅜ × 7½ in. [238 × 192 mm] folded at centre to 7½ × 4¹¹⁄₁₆ in. [192 × 119 mm]. Unnumbered. [1]: title page. [2]: blank. [3–4]: text. [5]: blank. [6]: text. [7]: blank. [8]: text. [9]: blank. [10]: text. [11]: blank. [12]: text. [13]: blank. [14]: text. [15]: blank. [16]: text. [17]: blank. [18]: text. [19]: blank. [20]: text. [21]: blank. [22]: text. [23]: blank. [24]: text. [25]: blank. [26–28]: text [answers to Nemo 1970]. [29]: text [marks and prizes, 1970]. [30]: text [remarks by John Fuller]. [31–32]: blank.

BACK COVER [line, 92 mm] | Printed for the Sycamore Press by Standard Press, Cirencester.

INSIDE FRONT [Calendar for 1971]

INSIDE BACK [Advertisement for Sycamore Press titles] | [Advertisement for book titled *Hide and Seek: Quotations and Questions from English Literature*]

BINDING Pale orange yellow (73) paper wraps bound with two staples.

PAPER Smooth white, unmarked.

NOTES Printed on 7 October 1970, in an edition of 350 copies by Standard Press for the Sycamore Press.

D6 **Advertisement for *Nemo's Almanac 1972* (1971)**

FRONT NEMO 1972 | [rule, 84 mm] | [in deep red (13)] Mr Keats opened the little volume and ruffled its |

pages with amusement. | "Nemo's Almanac," he inquired, "and what kind | of prognostications may one find here?" | Fanny was careful to blush. | "None, I declare. One is required to identify the | quotations from English Literature. It is really | very edifying." | "Is it, indeed?" Mr Keats smiled, and Fanny was | obliged yet again to observe closely how the dull | swain on her fan forever failed to catch the nymph | he pursued. Her interlocutor, who only half sus- | pected that she was flirting with him, persisted in | his close examination until she in truth began to | be weary of him. At last, when Mrs Brawne ann- | ounced a quadrille, Fanny was relieved to take the | arm of a convenient officer of the D—— regiment | leaving poor Mr Keats in the sole company of the | literary Almanac she had originally acquired, he | being a poet, if an ill-statured student of medicine, | in order to attract him. But he was too absorbed | to notice... | [in black; rule, 84 mm] | *Nemo's Almanac for 1972 is now available | (price 30p) from the Sycamore Press, | 4 Benson Place, Oxford.*

BACK   POST CARD | THE ADDRESS TO BE WRITTEN ON THIS SIDE [rectangle to upper right (23 × 19 mm)]

COLLATION   Single card measuring 5½ × 3½ in. [141 × 89 mm].

PAPER   Standard white postcard stock.

NOTES   Printed in September or early October 1971. Edition is not specified, but the press ledger indicates 125 cards were mailed on 6 October 1971.

D7   *Nemo's Almanac 1972*
(October 1971)

FRONT COVER   NEMO'S ALMANAC 1972 | *A literary competition in its 81st year* | [line, 120 mm] | "I believe you couldn't show me the | piece of English print, that I wouldn't | be equal to collaring and throwing." | [line, 120 mm] | Sycamore Press 30p

TITLE PAGE	[in double ruled box 92 × 35 mm] NEMO'S ALMANAC 1972 | *EDITED BY JOHN FULLER* | *Sycamore Press, 4 Benson Place, Oxford* | [competition rules] | [statement regarding marks and prizes]
IMPRINT PAGE	None.
COLLATION	Eight sheets 9⅞₁₆ × 7¼ in. [240 × 185 mm] folded at centre to 7¼ × 4¾ in. [185 × 120 mm]. Unnumbered. [1]: title page. [2]: blank. [3–4]: text. [5]: blank. [6]: text. [7]: blank. [8]: text. [9]: blank. [10]: text. [11]: blank. [12]: text. [13]: blank. [14]: text. [15]: blank. [16]: text. [17]: blank. [18]: text. [19]: blank. [20]: text. [21]: blank. [22]: text. [23]: blank. [24]: text. [25]: blank. [26–28]: text [answers to Nemo 1971]. [29]: text [marks and prizes, 1971]. [30–31]: text [remarks by John Fuller] | [Advertisement for book titled *Hide and Seek: Quotations and Questions from English Literature*]. [32]: [Advertising statement and order form for Sycamore Press publications].
BACK COVER	[line, 92 mm] | Printed for the Sycamore Press by Standard Press, Cirencester.
INSIDE FRONT	[Calendar for 1972]
INSIDE BACK	Blank.
BINDING	Light blue (181) paper wraps bound with two staples.
PAPER	Smooth white, unmarked.
NOTES	Printed on 13 October 1971, in an edition of 512 copies by Standard Press for the Sycamore Press.

D8   Advertisement for Sycamore Press Broadsheets (1971)

FRONT	Sycamore Broadsheets | [ten-line quotation] | (*The Poetry Review.* Autumn, 1970.) | 5p each, or make sure | you receive them as | they appear: 8 for 50p, | post free. | A few complete sets of the first twelve | broadsheets are available in a specially |

printed envelope for £3. Poets included | are Roy Fuller, James Fenton, Thom | Gunn and Peter Porter. | *Sycamore Press, 4 Benson Place, Oxford.*

BACK   Blank.

COLLATION   Single card measuring 5 × 3¹⁵⁄₁₆ in. [128 × 101 mm].

PAPER   Standard white postcard stock.

NOTES   Printed in late September or early October 1971. Edition is not specified in press ledger.

D9   **Advertisement for *Nemo's Almanac 1973***
            (October 1972)

FRONT   [within ornate box (46 × 78 mm.)] *You are invited to | try your hand at | Nemo's Almanac |* [below box] *The 1973 issue is now ready: 30p (or five for £1) plus postage | from John Fuller, Sycamore Press, 4 Benson Place, Oxford* [to the left of the box is an image of a hand pointing to the text within; the hand in deep blue (179)]

BACK   POST CARD | THE ADDRESS TO BE WRITTEN ON THIS SIDE [rectangle to upper right (23 × 19 mm)]

COLLATION   Single card measuring 5½ × 3½ in. [141 × 89 mm].

PAPER   Standard white postcard stock.

NOTES   Printed in October 1972. Edition is not specified, but the press ledger indicates 96 cards were mailed on 11 October 1972.

D10   ***Nemo's Almanac 1973***
            (October 1972)

FRONT COVER NEMO'S ALMANAC 1973 | *A literary competition in its 82nd year* | [line, 120 mm] | Even the Sycamore with her thousand | keys | Could not force locks as intricate as | theses, | nor Argus ravel out such mysteries. | [line, 120 mm] | Sycamore Press 30p

TITLE PAGE [in double ruled box 92 × 36 mm] NEMO'S ALMANAC 1973 | *EDITED BY JOHN FULLER*

| *Sycamore Press, 4 Benson Place, Oxford* |
[competition rules] | [statement regarding marks
and prizes]

IMPRINT PAGE None.

COLLATION Eight sheets 9⁷⁄₁₆ × 7¼ in. [240 × 185 mm] folded
at centre to 7¼ × 4¾ in. [185 × 120 mm].
Unnumbered. [1]: title page. [2]: blank. [3–4]:
text. [5]: blank. [6]: text. [7]: blank. [8]: text.
[9]: blank. [10]: text. [11]: blank. [12]: text. [13]:
blank. [14]: text. [15]: blank. [16]: text. [17]:
blank. [18]: text. [19]: blank. [20]: text. [21]:
blank. [22]: text. [23]: blank. [24]: text. [25]:
blank. [26–28]: text [answers to Nemo 1972].
[29]: text [marks and prizes, 1972]. [30–31]:
text [remarks by John Fuller] | [Advertisement
for book titled *Hide and Seek: Quotations
and Questions from English Literature*]. [32]:
[Advertising statement for Sycamore Press
publications].

BACK COVER [line, 92 mm] | Printed for the Sycamore Press by
Standard Press, Cirencester.

INSIDE FRONT [Calendar for 1973]

INSIDE BACK Blank.

BINDING Vivid red (11) paper wraps bound with two staples.

PAPER Smooth white, unmarked.

NOTES Printed on 10 October 1972, in an edition of 408
copies by Standard Press for the Sycamore Press.
In December 1972, an additional 100 copies were
produced by copying the text using Truexpress.
A block was made of the cover, which was then
printed on 'yellow Glastonbury wove' paper by
the Sycamore Press.

D11 **Advertisement for *Nemo's Almanac 1974***
(1973)

FRONT [image of a trellis to left, in dark yellowish green
(137)] | [in very dark red (17)] Alice then saw that
they were not roses at all, but pieces | of paper

with quotations on them. The Queen began pluck- | ing them eagerly and putting them in her little book. | "What grows all year and never reaches the top?" she | asked. Alice pondered. | "Of course," continued the Queen, consulting a Concord- | ance, "August is *such* a trying month. Wales! Venice!!" | Alice looked round, puzzled. | "It certainly isn't as green as it might be," she ventured | timidly. "Don't you have a gardener?" | "It isn't meant to be Green!" shrieked the Queen like an | express train. "By no means! And a Gardner is out of the | question. Have you guessed the riddle yet?" | "I haven't the faintest idea," replied Alice. | "Why, my *Nemo* entry, of course," said the Queen. | By this time, the trellis was completely bare. | [decorative rule, 95 mm] | Nemo's Almanac for 1974 is now ready: 35p | [four for £1, ten for £2] plus postage. from | John Fuller, Sycamore Press, 4 Benson Place | Oxford. Ideal for Christmas presents. Prizes.

BACK   POST CARD | THE ADDRESS TO BE WRITTEN ON THIS SIDE [rectangle to upper right (23 × 19 mm)]

COLLATION   Single card measuring 5½ × 3½ in. [141 × 89 mm].

PAPER   Standard white postcard stock.

NOTES   Printed in late September or early October 1973. Edition is not specified, but the press ledger indicates 180 cards were mailed on 10 October 1973.

D12   **Advertisement for *Truce* by David Harsent** (October 1973)

FRONT   [in dark yellowish green (137); rectangle made up of four lines of varying thickness (85 × 50 mm)] [within rectangle, in dark reddish brown (44)] DAVID HARSENT | [in dark yellowish green (137)] TRUCE | [in dark reddish brown (44)] Sycamore Press | [below rectangle, in dark reddish brown (44)] A new sequence of poems in a limited & | signed edition of two hundred copies | Sixteen pages in paper covers | Printed by hand at the Sycamore Press | 4 Benson Place, Oxford. Price: 60p

BACK   Blank.

COLLATION   Single card measuring 5 × 4 in. [128 × 103 mm].

PAPER   Standard white postcard stock.

NOTES   Printed in October 1973 in an edition of 75 copies.

D13   *Nemo's Almanac 1974*
(October 1973)

FRONT COVER   NEMO'S ALMANAC 1974 | *A literary competition in its 83rd year* | [line, 120 mm] | How easy is it for a man to fill | a book with quotations. | [line, 120 mm] | Sycamore Press 35p

TITLE PAGE   [in double ruled box 92 × 37 mm] NEMO'S ALMANAC 1974 | *EDITED BY JOHN FULLER* | *Sycamore Press, 4 Benson Place, Oxford* | [competition rules] | [statement regarding marks and prizes]

IMPRINT PAGE   None.

COLLATION   Eight sheets 9½ × 7¼ in. [242 × 185 mm] folded at centre to 7¼ × 4¾ in. [185 × 121 mm]. Unnumbered. [1]: title page. [2]: blank. [3-4]: text. [5]: blank. [6]: text. [7]: blank. [8]: text. [9]: blank. [10]: text. [11]: blank. [12]: text. [13]: blank. [14]: text. [15]: blank. [16]: text. [17]: blank. [18]: text. [19]: blank. [20]: text. [21]: blank. [22]: text. [23]: blank. [24]: text. [25]: blank. [26-28]: text [answers to Nemo 1973]. [29]: text [marks and prizes, 1973]. [30-31]: text [remarks by John Fuller]. [32]: text [additional remarks by Fuller under the heading of 'Oddments', including advertising statements for Sycamore Press publications].

BACK COVER   [line, 92 mm] | Printed for the Sycamore Press by F. Bailey & Son Ltd., Dursley, Glos.

INSIDE FRONT	[Calendar for 1974]
INSIDE BACK	Blank.
BINDING	Light green (144) paper wraps bound with two staples.
PAPER	Smooth white, unmarked.
NOTES	Printed on 9 October 1973, in an edition of 623 copies by F. Bailey & Son for the Sycamore Press.

D14 Advertisement for *Nemo's Almanac 1975* (1974)

FRONT	Nemo's Almanac for 1975 is now ready: 40p	[four for £1] and postage, from John Fuller,	Sycamore Press, 4 Benson Place, Oxford.	Prizes. Ideal for Christmas presents.	[in block letters to background and filling entire face of card, in moderate blue (182)] NEMO
BACK	POST CARD	THE ADDRESS TO BE WRITTEN ON THIS SIDE [rectangle to upper right (23 × 19 mm)]
COLLATION	Single card measuring 5½ × 3½ in. [141 × 89 mm].
PAPER	Standard white postcard stock.
NOTES	Printed in September or early October 1974. Edition is not specified, but the press ledger indicates 150 cards were purchased for publicity purposes on 8 September 1974.

D15 *Nemo's Almanac 1975* (October 1974)

FRONT COVER	NEMO'S ALMANAC 1975	*A literary competition in its 84th year*	[line, 122 mm]	And rhymes appropriate could make	To ev'ry month i' th' almanack	[line, 122 mm]	Sycamore Press 40p
TITLE PAGE	[in double ruled box 92 × 37 mm] NEMO'S ALMANAC 1975	*EDITED BY JOHN FULLER*	*Sycamore Press, 4 Benson Place, Oxford*	

	[competition rules]	[statement regarding marks and prizes]
IMPRINT PAGE	None.
COLLATION	Eight sheets 9½ × 7¼ in. [242 × 185 mm] folded at centre to 7¼ × 4¾ in. [185 × 121 mm]. Unnumbered. [1]: title page. [2]: blank. [3–4]: text. [5]: blank. [6]: text. [7]: blank. [8]: text. [9]: blank. [10]: text. [11]: blank. [12]: text. [13]: blank. [14]: text. [15]: blank. [16]: text. [17]: blank. [18]: text. [19]: blank. [20]: text. [21]: blank. [22]: text. [23]: blank. [24]: text. [25]: blank. [26–28]: text [answers to Nemo 1974]. [29]: text [marks and prizes, 1974]. [30]: text [remarks by John Fuller]. [31]: text [adverts and queries under the heading of 'Oddments', including advertising statements for Sycamore Press publications]. [32]: [headed 'Readers' Notes', otherwise blank].
BACK COVER	[line, 93 mm]	Printed for the Sycamore Press by F. Bailey & Son Ltd., Dursley	Glos.
INSIDE FRONT	[Calendar for 1975]
INSIDE BACK	Blank.
BINDING	Pale orange yellow (73) paper wraps bound with two staples.
PAPER	Smooth white, unmarked.
NOTES	Printed in an edition of 619 copies by F. Bailey & Son for the Sycamore Press [printing consisted of 626 copies, but 7 were misbound]. In November 1974, an additional 400 copies were produced by copying the text using Truexpress. A block was made of the cover, which was then printed by the Sycamore Press.

D16 Advertisement for *Nemo's Almanac 1976* (September 1975)

| FRONT | [in dark blue (183)] Q: what is grey, wrinkled and heavy? | [printed upside down] A: a Nemo competitor's brain. | I'm sneaking this reminder |

card out before the rise in postage rates, | but by the time you've sent me your cheque or postal order *Nemo's* | *Almanac* for 1976 will be ready. 50p a copy, or £1.50 for four ($1.75 | or $4.50), from John Fuller, 4 Benson Place, Oxford, England. | [image of an elephant to background and filling entire face of card, in light grey (264)]

BACK   POST CARD | THE ADDRESS TO BE WRITTEN ON THIS SIDE [rectangle to upper right (23 × 19 mm)]

COLLATION   Single card measuring 5½ × 3½ in. [141 × 89 mm].

PAPER   Standard white postcard stock.

NOTES   Printed in September 1975. Edition is not specified, but the press ledger indicates 280 cards were purchased for publicity purposes on 17 September 1974.

D17   *Nemo's Almanac 1976*
(October 1975)

FRONT COVER   NEMO'S ALMANAC 1976 | *A literary competition in its 85th year* | [line, 122 mm] | "A book that furnishes no quotations is, | *me judice*, no book—it is a plaything." | [line, 122 mm] | Sycamore Press 50p

TITLE PAGE   [in double ruled box 92 × 37 mm] NEMO'S ALMANAC 1976 | EDITED BY JOHN FULLER | Sycamore Press, 4 Benson Place, Oxford | [competition rules]

IMPRINT PAGE   None.

COLLATION   Eight sheets 9½ × 7¼ in. [242 × 185 mm] folded at centre to 7¼ × 4¾ in. [185 × 121 mm]. Unnumbered. [1]: title page. [2]: blank. [3–4]: text. [5]: blank. [6]: text. [7]: blank. [8]: text. [9]: blank. [10]: text. [11]: blank. [12]: text. [13]: blank. [14]: text. [15]: blank. [16]: text. [17]: blank. [18]: text. [19]: blank. [20]: text. [21]: blank. [22]: text. [23]: blank. [24]: text. [25]: blank. [26–28]: text [answers to Nemo 1975].

[29–30]: text [marks and prizes, 1975]. [31]: text
[remarks by John Fuller]. [32]: [headed 'Readers'
Notes', otherwise blank].

BACK COVER [line, 93 mm] | Printed for the Sycamore Press by F.
Bailey & Son Ltd., Dursley, | Glos.

INSIDE FRONT [Calendar for 1976]

INSIDE BACK [Adverts and queries under the heading of
'Oddments', including advertising statements for
Sycamore Press publications].

BINDING Vivid red (11) paper wraps bound with two staples.

PAPER Smooth white, unmarked.

NOTES Printed in an edition of 1,120 copies by F. Bailey &
Son for the Sycamore Press.

D18 **Advertisement for _Nemo's Almanac 1977_**
(1976)

FRONT [in very deep red (14); four rules of varying
thickness, 127 mm] | [centred between two block
images (25 × 28 mm.)] _You are invited to_ | _try_
your hand at | _Nemo's Almanac_ | [below images]
The 1977 Nemo's Almanac is ready! Newcomers:
dare | you waste your year identifying 73
quotations set in | months by themes, including
kisses, doors, bagpipes, | Oxford, breasts,
and the shortest chapters in English | fiction?
Old hands: find out the answers & the prize- |
winners! 50p or $1.50 each (£1.50 or $3.50 for
4 copies) | from John Fuller, 4 Benson Place,
Oxford, England. | [four rules of varying
thickness, 127 mm]

BACK POST CARD | THE ADDRESS TO BE WRITTEN
ON THIS SIDE [rectangle to upper right (23 × 19
mm)]

COLLATION Single card measuring 5½ × 3½ in. [141 × 89 mm].

PAPER Standard white postcard stock.

NOTES Printed in late September or early October 1976.
Edition is not specified, but the press ledger

indicates 400 cards were purchased for publicity purposes on 30 September 1975.

D19   *Nemo's Almanac 1977*
(October 1976)

FRONT COVER   NEMO'S ALMANAC 1977 | *A literary competition in its 86th year* | [line, 120 mm] | Nothing will please some Men, but | Books stuff'd with Antiquity, groaning | under the weight of Learned Quotations | [line, 120 mm] | Sycamore Press 50p

TITLE PAGE   [in double ruled box 93 × 38 mm] NEMO'S ALMANAC 1977 | EDITED BY JOHN FULLER | Sycamore Press, 4 Benson Place, Oxford | [competition rules]

IMPRINT PAGE   None.

COLLATION   Eight sheets 9⁷⁄₁₆ × 7¼ in. [240 × 185 mm] folded at centre to 7¼ × 4¾ in. [185 × 120 mm]. Unnumbered. [1]: title page. [2]: blank. [3–4]: text. [5]: blank. [6]: text. [7]: blank. [8]: text. [9]: blank. [10]: text. [11]: blank. [12]: text. [13]: blank. [14]: text. [15]: blank. [16]: text. [17]: blank. [18]: text. [19]: blank. [20]: text. [21]: blank. [22]: text. [23]: blank. [24]: text. [25]: blank. [26–28]: text [answers to Nemo 1976]. [29–31]: text [marks and prizes, 1976]. [32]: text [remarks by John Fuller].

BACK COVER   [line, 92 mm] | Printed for the Sycamore Press by F. Bailey & Son Ltd., Dursley, | Glos.

INSIDE FRONT   [Calendar for 1977]

INSIDE BACK   [headed 'Readers' Notes', otherwise blank]

BINDING   Brilliant yellow (83) paper wraps bound with two staples.

PAPER   Smooth white, unmarked.

NOTES   Printed in an edition of 1,235 copies by F. Bailey & Son Ltd for the Sycamore Press. (Ledger states payment was made to Standard Press.)

D20   **Advertisement for *Nemo's Almanac 1978***
(1977)

FRONT   [in dark yellowish green (137)] Nemo's Almanac
1978 | [image of chain links, 128 mm] | It's ready,
and with the usual mysteries! Who is the | Duke
of Puke? Why was the snake happy? Where |
does Dagon wed with Mother Carey? Why is
bacon | early, and what does lettuce have to do
with sleep? | You know you can't resist it, even
if you swore you'd | never do it again. What's
more, there are all the ans- | wers to the 1977
Almanac. And of course, 73 fresh | quotations
to be identified, set in monthly themes | such as
mountains, wind, American food, women's | pets,
and amphibiousness. Price: 60p or $1.60 each
| (£1.80 or $3.70 for four copies) post free from
John | Fuller, 4 Benson Place, Summertown,
Oxford.

BACK   POST CARD | THE ADDRESS TO BE WRITTEN
ON THIS SIDE [rectangle to upper right (23 × 19
mm)]

COLLATION   Single card measuring 5½ × 3½ in. [141 × 89 mm].

PAPER   Standard white postcard stock.

NOTES   Printed in September or October 1977. Edition is
not specified in ledger.

D21   *Nemo's Almanac 1978*
(1977)

FRONT COVER   NEMO'S ALMANAC 1978 | *A literary competition in
its 87th year* | [line, 120 mm] | A man will turn
over half a library to | make one book | [line, 120
mm] | Sycamore Press 60p

TITLE PAGE   [in double ruled box 93 × 38 mm] NEMO'S
ALMANAC 1978 | EDITED BY JOHN FULLER
| Sycamore Press, 4 Benson Place, Oxford |
[competition rules]

IMPRINT PAGE   None.

COLLATION   Eight sheets 9⅞₁₆ × 7¼ in. [240 × 185 mm] folded
at centre to 7¼ × 4¾ in. [185 × 120 mm].
Unnumbered. [1]: title page. [2]: blank. [3–4]:
text. [5]: blank. [6]: text. [7]: blank. [8]: text.
[9]: blank. [10]: text. [11]: blank. [12]: text. [13]:
blank. [14]: text. [15]: blank. [16]: text. [17]:
blank. [18]: text. [19]: blank. [20]: text. [21]:
blank. [22]: text. [23]: blank. [24]: text. [25]:
blank. [26–28]: text [answers to Nemo 1977].
[29–31]: text [marks and prizes, 1977]. [32]: text
[remarks by John Fuller].

BACK COVER   [line, 93 mm] | Printed for the Sycamore Press by
F. Bailey & Son Ltd., Dursley, | Glos.

INSIDE FRONT   [Calendar for 1978]

INSIDE BACK   [9 lines of text making up the end of the editor's
remarks] | [line, 92 mm] | *Readers' Notes* | [line,
92 mm]

BINDING   Very pale blue (184) paper wraps bound with two
staples.

PAPER   Smooth white, unmarked.

NOTES   Printed in an edition of 1,200 copies by F. Bailey &
Son Ltd for the Sycamore Press.

D22   **Advertisement for *Nemo's Almanac 1979***
(1978)

FRONT   [in dark blue (183)] OMEN! | The 1979 Nemo's
Almanac is now ready! Who is Mr. | Edward
Albert Tewler? Cudjo? John Lookye? Who | had
the favourite at Bowie? Who kept bees in Bath? |
Who heard the weak-ey'd Bat? This year we have
money, cows and success; Shakespeare, numbers
and | dancing; thought, Christmas and rivers;
pheasants, | evening and owls. 73 quotations,
bigger prizes, last | year's answers and (wait for
it) the price is the same. | Send 60p or $1.75
(£1.80 or $4 for four copies) to John | Fuller, 4
Benson Place, Summertown, Oxford.

BACK	POST CARD | THE ADDRESS TO BE WRITTEN ON THIS SIDE [rectangle to upper right (23 × 19 mm)]
COLLATION	Single card measuring 5½ × 3½ in. [141 × 89 mm]/
PAPER	Standard white postcard stock.
NOTES	Printed in 1978 in an unspecified number of copies.

D23   Advertisement for *Nemo's Almanac 1982* (1981)

FRONT	[to left side] NEMO | Identify | quotations | and keep | off the | grass… | [image of hand pointing to the right (16 × 36 mm)] | [to the right, a large image in Egyptian style (53 × 97 mm)] | [below image] *Nebuchadnezzar rushes to buy Nemo's Almanac 582 B.C.* | [decorative rule, 127 mm] | The 1982 Nemo's Almanac is now ready! Send £1 or | $4 [£3 or $8 for four copies] to John Fuller, 4 Benson | Place, Oxford OX2 6QH, England. [five floret images, 4 × 4 mm]
BACK	POST CARD | THE ADDRESS TO BE WRITTEN ON THIS SIDE [rectangle to upper right (23 × 19 mm)]
COLLATION	Single card measuring 5½ × 3½ in. [141 × 89 mm].
PAPER	Standard white postcard stock.
NOTES	Printed in 1981 in an unspecified number of copies.

D24   Advertisement for *Nemo's Almanac 1983* (1982)

FRONT	[to left side, silhouette image of two men talking, the left with a cane] [to right of image] NEMO | B: 'But, Sir, is not the identifying | of quotations (and for gain) an idle | occupation for a man of learning?' | J: 'You are wrong, Sir. Nemo's | Almanac is the only book that has | ever taken me out of bed two hours | sooner than I wished to rise. It is a | drug, Sir, and drugs are sometimes

| necessary.' | [decorative rule, 127 mm] | The 1983 Nemo's Almanac is now ready! Send £1 or | $4 [£3 or $8 for four copies] to John Fuller, 4 Benson | Place, Oxford OX2 6QH, England. [five floret images, 4 × 4 mm]

BACK   POST CARD | THE ADDRESS TO BE WRITTEN ON THIS SIDE [rectangle to upper right (23 × 19 mm)]

COLLATION   Single card measuring 5½ × 3½ in. [141 × 89 mm].

PAPER   Standard white postcard stock.

NOTES   Printed in 1982 in an unspecified number of copies.

D25   **Advertisement for *Nemo's Almanac 1985*** (1984)

FRONT   [in vivid red (11)] [to left side, image of two men playing rugby] [to right of image] Are you ready to tackle the | celebrated quotations game, | NEMO'S ALMANAC? | [decorative rule, 118 mm] | The 1985 edition is now ready. One copy for | £1.20 (or $5 by air), four copies for £3.75 ($10). | John Fuller, 4 Benson Place, Oxford OX2 6QH

BACK   POST CARD | THE ADDRESS TO BE WRITTEN ON THIS SIDE [rectangle to upper right (23 × 19 mm)]

COLLATION   Single card measuring 5½ × 3½ in. [141 × 89 mm].

PAPER   Standard white postcard stock.

NOTES   Printed in 1984 in an unspecified number of copies.

Newsletters & ephemera

E1   **Poems from Lumb Bank** (October 1982)

FRONT   [in deep red (13)] [within decorative rule border] POEMS | from | LUMB | BANK | [rule] | [ornament] | October | 1982

TITLE PAGE	POEMS FROM LUMB BANK | October 1982
IMPRINT PAGE	Most of these poems were written or | completed at an Arvon Foundation | poetry course at Lumb Bank between | 27 September and 2 October 1982.
COLLATION	Four sheets measuring 10⅞ × 8³⁄₁₆ in. [276 × 208 mm] folded at centre to 8³⁄₁₆ × 5⁷⁄₁₆ in. [208 × 138 mm]. Unnumbered. [1]: title page. [2]: imprint page. [3–16]: text.
BACK COVER	Blank.
BINDING	Light grey (264) paper wraps stapled.
PAPER	Standard white; no watermark.
NOTES	Includes a poem by John Fuller titled 'The Mountain and the Pool'. Regarding this pamphlet, Fuller writes, '*Poems from Lumb Bank* was produced at a week-long Arvon Foundation course that I taught with Laurence Lerner at Lumb Bank (a house in Brontë country owned by Ted Hughes, and leased to the Foundation). I had taught such a course before, and anticipated that we might be able to produce a booklet of the poems that the students (and their tutors!) wrote during the week. I therefore ran off a small number of covers on the press and took them up with me to Yorkshire. I stayed up half the night typing out and cyclostyling the poems and then folding and stabbing them into the covers. Not a Sycamore Press item, of course, but an associated thing, I suppose.'

E2	**Publicity flyer** (2 January 1983)
COLLATION	Single sheet folded twice to form six unnumbered panels.
PAPER	Standard white A4 paper.
CONTENTS	Contains reviews for Mick Imlah's *The Zoologist's Bath and Other Adventures*, an advert for Nemo's

Almanac, and a list of additional Sycamore Press titles available for purchase.

NOTES Text is typed or clipped from other publications and copied, not set on the press.

E3 **John Florio Society Dinner**
(2 December 1987)

FRONT [in vivid red (11)] THE JOHN FLORIO SOCIETY | DINNER | "Kissing don't last: cookery do!" | [large ornament] | 2 December 1982

COLLATION Single sheet measuring 11⅝ × 8¼ in. [296 × 210 mm] folded at centre to 8¼ × 5¹³⁄₁₆ in. [210 × 148 mm].

BACK COVER [in vivid red (11)] [image of two men, the left with a cane] | "A man is in general better pleased when he has a good | dinner upon his table, than when his wife talks Greek."

PAPER Brilliant orange yellow (67), single sheet folded.

NOTES All text, including interior menu in vivid red (11). Of this, John Fuller writes, 'The menu for the Florio Society dinner is self-explanatory, I think. The unascribed quotation on the cover is from Meredith.'

E4 **Newsletter 2**
(December 1989)

COLLATION Single sheet, folded at centre to form four unnumbered pages.

PAPER Standard white A4 paper.

CONTENTS Announces the publication of Gerard Woodward's *The Unwriter and other poems.* Also lists additional poetry pamphlets still available from the press. Announces a poetry reading 'planned for Ash Wednesday, 28 February 1990 in the Summer Common Room of Magdalen College, Oxford, at 8.00' at which a number of Sycamore Press poets will read their works.

NOTES   Text is typed and copied, not set on the press.

E5   **Newsletter 3 + Catalogue**
       (October 1992)

COLLATION   Single sheet folded at centre to form four
       unnumbered pages.

PAPER   Standard white A4 paper.

CONTENTS   Announces the closing of the press and offers
       remaining unsold copies of various Sycamore
       Press items.

NOTES   Text is typed and copied, not set on the press.

Index